# HACKING

## —THE—

# HOLY GRAIL

### THE TRADER'S GUIDE TO CRACKING
### THE CODE OF PROFITABILITY

Authored by Doc Severson
Illustrated by Charmaine Severson
Published by Createspace

**Hacking the Holy Grail:**

The Trader's Guide to Cracking the Code of Profitability

# Dedication

To my wife Maureen: Thank you my love for your constant encouragement, and joy of the Journey which we share.

To my kids Charlie, Will, and Ellie....you've helped me "Go the Distance."

And to Gramps.... for the inspiration and the Pocket Protectors.

# Table Of Contents

# Preface

Let's get one thing straight from the beginning; I am not a doctor. I am not a licensed medical doctor, nor do I hold a PhD. I hold the utmost respect for those that have dedicated their lives to intense and specific study to earn that title of "Doctor," so it's with some humility and trepidation that I offer myself to the reader as "Doc." This is a nickname that has been affixed to me for decades, perhaps at first by the similarity to the name of Johnny Carson's bandleader Doc Severinsen (although our last names are pronounced very differently), but as co-workers and friends have gotten to know me and my mannerisms, the nickname became more of a salute to my "bedside manner" and thought process. I like to find the source of the pain in people's lives and fix the problem so that the pain goes away.

You see, I always wanted to be a doctor, from the time that I knew that Medicine was a profession. I would proudly proclaim to anyone that would listen, "I'm going to be a Doctor when I grow up!" I clearly remember bringing general anatomy books to study in the classroom when I was in first grade, and it was a wonderful pursuit and goal to strive for. Well, that all came crashing down a few years later when I nearly passed out filleting a catfish (Who would not stop wiggling even without a head), and what sealed it for me was finding out that I would not be out of school until the advanced age of THIRTY, which is the age that I believed that one already had a foot in the grave. Perhaps some timely counseling would have kept me on track, but I quickly acquired a new life goal and that was Electronics and the application of technology.

Fast forward to today; after a few flirtations with going back to Medical School at various "too-late" stages of my life, I've been able to channel my natural desire to "heal" into something a little less gory, but something equally important to people: Financial freedom for individuals. There is probably not a single pursuit that offers the amount of blinding promise as the stock market does....yet it comes with an absolutely confounding array of behaviors that often dash our dreams. And as we'll see, many of the methods and attitudes that made us successful in business, or any other aspect of life....work proportionally against us in this new venture of financial markets.

I won't be so presumptuous as to suggest that I can solve all of your financial pain, but what I hope to achieve in this book is: 1) to show you how much you already know, and 2) the hope that you will find just one nugget within these pages that might push you over the top of the hill, and into easier times for you. Sometimes all it takes is one little push.

Any personal examples used in this book are either imaginary, or their names have been changed because the point is important, not the specific name. So there.

Doc Severson

September 2015

# Introduction:
## The Pull of Mediocrity

What has happened to the "American Dream" of the twentieth century? You know, the one where June and Ward buy the house with the white picket fence, raise 2.6 kids and a dog or two, retire at age 65 with a golden pension and lifetime benefits, and retire to golf away the rest of their lives in Sun City, AZ? You don't have to look far around you to see that "dream" is rapidly turning into vapor all around us. Americans simply aren't prepared for retirement, and can't save anything because they are working paycheck-to-paycheck. The results of one study shows us that the median value of retirement savings for those aged 55 to 64 is just $103,000[i]. Combine that with another study that shows that retirement medical costs for a couple will run $220,000[ii] , and you can see how daunting a challenge that this appears to be for most folks approaching retirement. The numbers just don't add up.

Well, that's OK, that's what Social Security is for, right? Think again. Social Security payments, on average, only accounted for $1300/month of income in 2014[iii] , meaning that most are looking at a fixed income of less than $20,000/year to get through what are supposed to be their "Golden Years." Is it any wonder why increasing numbers of retirees have to move in with extended family just to survive? To make ends meet, many are turning to "reverse mortgages" which allows them to withdrawal a part of their home equity as cash income, tax-free. Just another example of a crumbling foundation, as something that couples have invested in throughout their adult lives is being turned into a liability again.

You might be reading this, thinking to yourself "Yes, I feel bad for those retirees, but what about ME!? I'm forty years old, have no retirement savings, and I'm struggling just to survive!" More and more I'm seeing the symbols of decay in this society, with TV commercials featuring well-known celebrities hawking short-term "payday" loans, or other services offering "fast cash NOW!" In fact, recently I've noticed that where I live in Middle America, I can't drive past a strip mall without seeing "payday loan" and "title loan" storefronts. Here we have people who are using their car titles as collateral to get a short-term loan just to survive.

**Temporary America** - typical retail strip showing title loan, pay-day loan, and rental furniture all in one conveniently miserable location.

Is it any wonder that we have more disenfranchised citizens running around rioting, burning flags, and committing crimes than seemingly ever before? None of these situations that I've just described are the foundation for a strong economy or a stable lifestyle, whether they are working, unemployed, or retired. And it's just getting worse in front of our eyes while politicians claim that we're in a "strong recovery."

I was trained as an engineer; I solve problems. Let's find out why this is happening, and what we can do to fix it.

## Why Is This Happening?

I should warn you ahead of time that the following are my opinions, analysis, and suggestions; if you're easily offended or if you've already made up your mind as to why this is happening to us and how to fix it, then simply move to the first chapter.

A look around you or a quick glance at the papers or headline news will show you that not everyone has been afflicted by this malaise; in fact, quite the opposite. A small percentage of Americans have become richer than ever. Agitators have referred to these folks as "one-percenters" as they represent the top one-percent of wage earners. In rough numbers, it takes about $400k of annual gross revenue[iv] to hit this club. While this is quite a distance from the Average Annual Mean Income of Americans of about $50,000, earning $400k in the US does not make you "rich" and is likely a small business revenue figure before expenses and taxes are removed. So then, what is the problem with these "One-Percenters?"

**Problem Number One** - Those in the "One-Percenter" club have been identified as villains in today's society, and media is making it "uncool" to be successful.

What happened to "The Land of Opportunity?" The way that people treat others is a reflection of how they feel about themselves. Those that are not taking advantage of the opportunities of being in the United States (we'll get to WHY in a minute) are going to point at people who HAVE figured it out, and try to tear them down.

OK, if those at the top have it figured out and have increased the "gap" between themselves and the Median, what's happened to the "middle" of the income curve to cause this disparity to become so obvious? Popular media tends to once again miss the mark, focusing on CEO pay with their eight-figure salaries and huge golden parachutes. Yep, more "bad guys" to demonize. While CEO pay can be ridiculous for some, don't forget that we're talking about a VERY small subset of people here. Accordingly, the media also focuses on the other side of the distribution curve, those making minimum wage and how $10/hour is "unfair" to those working fast food. Once again, we're collectively missing the point. What about the middle of the bell curve? This is where the majority of wage earners are, generating the bulk of the US Income. Where has the middle class gone? CHINA. Take a walk through any Wal-Mart or other "superstore" and tell me where the products are being made? Yes, China. The unbreakable laws of supply and demand have disrupted the former giant of US Industry. Labor costs to produce a product in the US are higher than outsourcing it to China and then shipping it across the Pacific. But honestly, hasn't this been happening for a LONG time? Those who are over 50 can remember when they'd read "Made in Japan" on all of the toys, and it was just as prevalent as "Made in China" is today.

But beyond outsourcing manufacturing, something else which has killed jobs in the middle class is Automation. Who needs a bank teller when you can go to an ATM? Who needs a gas station attendant when you can pump your own gas? What began as a hyped-up promise in the late 1990's regarding the Internet….has fulfilled its reality in becoming an automation and distribution channel….but at the same time, displacing those that used to manually perform those roles. Think about this for a second…. Facebook's 2014 revenues were over 12.5 Billion dollars, and they only employed slightly over 6000 employees. Compare that with General Motors which required 202,000 people to produce $156 Billion in revenue, at a much lower profit margin and slower growth. Today's technologies that generate services do not require a lot of human capital to run.  OK, let's wrap this up into a problem statement:

**Problem Number Two** - The US economy no longer requires the same roles from human "labor" that it once did due to supply/demand shifts and advances in technology.

What we've identified so far is that the ground has "shifted" but someone's still making money so they must be the bad people, those "One-Percenters" that I referenced above. Unfortunately, now we get to the "ideology" part of the discussion. The United States was founded to be this "land of liberty" where you could pretty much do anything you want as long as you didn't tread on others, protected by the Bill of Rights. It was always positioned as the Land of Opportunity where you could start with nothing and work your way to success. And this is still true; ask any immigrant who has taken huge risks to come to this country and become a citizen. And, quite frankly, those who have been paying attention to the changes in society and technology have found no lack of opportunity, REGARDLESS of their backgrounds. This is still that land of opportunity, yet for the reasons that I've laid out above, many are either unaware of the changes or are simply expecting to keep doing the same thing while expecting different results.

So why do some folks "get it" and the vast majority does not? Is there some magic gene splicing experiment that occurred which allows some folks to anticipate the future and profit from it? Or is the population just inherently lazy and we'd rather keep up with the Kardashians? As usual, the answer lies somewhere in between. I think that one of the most obvious failings is with the Education system; we are still training children to take tests instead of teaching them how to function in the real world. We hear administrators brag about how an education in the Arts will "broaden" one's outlook, yet these same kids can't balance a checkbook and have chained themselves with six figures of student debt, many of them unable to find employment with their double major of Biology and Brazilian Art History. Please don't get me wrong, I love the Arts and the older I get, the more I appreciate the subtleties of life that the Arts give us. But kids in their twenties need to become productive members of society and need to find employment. Too often, the Education system creates an inbred mentality. "I can't find a job in the evil corporate world so I'll just stay in college and get my PhD and then teach."

At the other end of the educational spectrum you have a very efficient Engineering/Accounting/Legal educational machine that is spitting out and employing these professionals as fast as it can accept and grind them through the system. These kids are gainfully employed but so busy automating, counting, and litigating everything that moves at light speed, everyone else has been left behind. Very few of these employed really understand the function and value of "business" beyond their own functional silo.

So let's wrap this up into the next major issue:

**Problem Number Three** - The Education system is not teaching children how to create value, stay up with the pace of change, and conduct business in the most entrepreneurial country on the planet. Our education system is still grounded in the "Organization Man" principles of the 1950's, not the hyper-speed world of the new millennium where concepts are evolving in days, not years.

Now, because of the fact that the Educational system has led literally millions of individuals down this primrose path with a sour ending, you have a huge problem with graduates unable to find a job, unable to create a career, and have to move back in to their Parents' home (Who are having their own issues staring at Retirement!). Who's at fault? Well, it's those EVIL corporations that won't give me a job! It's those lousy One-Percenters that are hogging all of the money! Let's Occupy Wall Street and burn down their houses!

When you have this type of fertile ground, just add a group of folks that want to change the dynamics in the United States to that of a more "socialist" state, and you have a combustible situation. They are using the afore-mentioned titanic shifts in automation and supply/demand as a wedge against those not doing as well…. to get to what they want, which is ultimately power. Their message is very appealing; let "US, THE GOVERNMENT" take care of things, it's not your fault, you shouldn't have to work as hard, we'll put a bigger burden on those nasty One-Percenters, just vote for me and we'll give you all of that "stuff." So this brings me to my fourth identifiable problem with the financial health of today's society, which is "class warfare for votes:"

**Problem Number Four** - The overwhelming message communicated by politicians and media is that you don't have to take personal responsibility for your own future, because we'll make those "bad guys" pay their "fair share" for it. Just vote us into office and we'll make the pain go away, while we accumulate power.

So there we have it. The fabric of society is crumbling, and with it the economy. The role of the worker has changed dramatically in the last 15 years. There are no more cushy corporate jobs; everyone is a Free Agent now.

We're not being taught to anticipate and deal with the changes happening to the workforce; by the time they see it, it's too late.

We're being rewarded for playing the Victim mentality.

We can either choose to lay back and remain with the disgruntled herd, or do something about it.

## What Can We Do About It?

Well, I'm glad you're still with me. Frankly, it's not my concern whether or not you agree with me on all the points I've made above. I've tried to keep the usual partisan politics out of this, because they just cloud the issue and make people resistant to adopting ideas. (My team is better than your team!) My only concern is that you DO AGREE that changes need to be made.

Now, I'm not going to change the world with this book, but what I do want to change is YOUR AP-PROACH, one investor at a time.

Can anyone in the United States still become a successful "One-Percenter?" Of course. (Or for that matter, any country with a similar economic and political structure)

Do YOU want to become a successful "One-Percenter?" That's entirely up to you. If you believe at your core that they are evil, greedy people, then we are going to face more challenges getting you to a mind-set of "abundance."

Do YOU want to create a more stable retirement income? A more livable working income, if you are younger? All of these desires are possible.

To start with, I am going to need you to tackle those four issues head-on. Let's get started:

1. **Success** - I need you to have a burning desire to be successful, without a shred of doubt in your mind. If your mind is clouded that successful people are greedy and undeserving, then you're going to make things much more difficult for yourself down the road. We'll discuss ways of dealing with that later, but for now we will not be able to make any progress if there is the least shred of doubt in your mind that being successful would be absolutely fantastic.

2. **Evolve** - You need to look at the future as an opportunity to do things differently, and not bemoan the fact that the past is gone. The future belongs to those that embrace and define it, and not to those that are continually trying to make the future resemble the past. This is a chance to break the bonds of the past and re-invent yourself. Do you feel excited by this possibility, or apprehensive? Change is difficult, but you need to learn to embrace and excel in change if you are to be successful in the new normal.

3. **Learning** - You will need to become a learning machine. With the speed of change and evolu-

tion comes the responsibility to adapt quickly. The US Marine Corps has a saying, "Improvise, Adapt, and Overcome." This means that what you experience on a daily basis will not have a solution in some manual, but rather will be based on your ability to use your founding principles and logical thought process to creatively devise a solution. And this will be based on your ability to learn on the spot as you adapt to a rapidly changing world.

4. **Accountability and Personal Responsibility** - I don't know about you, but I'm not counting on Social Security to be around when I need it. And with potential "means testing" being floated as a way to keep this system solvent, my goal is to pass my stash along to someone else that truly needs it. I look at earlier generations who would do ANYTHING but take unemployment benefits, and now it's just a punchbowl. I want you to take ACCOUNTABILITY for all of your actions, and I want you to assume that this is the MOST important thing that you'll need to master.

And now that I've got you fired up, I'd like to present a short story to you in the first few chapters of this book. I think that this is a story that you'll find familiar in many ways, so my goal is to make it relatable. See you at the end of the story...

## Chapter One:
# The Trials of Percy

"Good thing that house doesn't have lath and plaster walls" Percy thinks to himself numbly, as he wanders the aisles at the local home improvement warehouse, barely keeping his mind on task. He scans the shelves, left and right, left and right, looking for something....but not really looking. His mind is elsewhere.

"Can I help you find something?" booms a voice, shocking him back to reality. A large, smiling man with an apron and a name tag labeled "Jim" stands in front of him. "Oh...uh, yeah" mumbles Percy. "I'm trying to patch a hole in my wall."

"A hole in your wall? Well, how big is it and what type of wall is it?" asks Jim. Percy stares at his feet, looks left...then right...oddly avoiding Jim's gaze. "Oh, about a foot wide, and I think it's regular dry-wall." Jim notices Percy's odd reaction, but decides to let it go at that, and not probe any further. "Follow me, and I'll show you what you need" states Jim as he leads him to aisle 23 and "Building Supplies." An hour later Percy is home again, tending to his weekend errands, yet his mind is already fast-forwarding to Monday, and wondering what his next step was going to be.

It was about a year ago that this all started. Percy Hedger, Senior Program Manager for CubEx software, was sitting through another intolerable meeting where nothing was getting done. Percy made a comfortable salary, yet for some reason his finances were paycheck-to-paycheck. With all of the demands of life and family, a mountain of debt was the result of trying to provide the life he felt that his wife Jenna and their two kids deserved. An average suburban home in Houston, two car payments, braces for his daughter, and mounting credit card debt left him little to work with at the end of every month. College tuition was right around the corner for their oldest child, and Jenna was dropping hints about quitting her job as a dental receptionist. "How the hell do you get ahead in this world?" Percy wondered to himself, distracted and daydreaming through the staff meeting.

And then it hit the fan...."Hey Percy, can you give us an update on the upcoming software release?" asked his division VP. "Oh crap!" was the only thing running through his mind, as he scrambled to think of what he could say. "Well, we're about a month behind our target date, but I think we can bring that in

by a week" Percy blurted. "WHAT?!" cried the VP…
"We've already promised that module to GE next
week!" The rest of the meeting dissolved into a blur
of back-and-forth responses and Percy felt like everyone's eyes were burning holes into the back of his
skull. Another late night, and he'd promised to take
his wife Jenna out to dinner that evening. To his relief, the staff meeting finally broke up, and Percy re-
treated to the safety of his office and closed the door.

Once the door closed and he sat at his desk, his head
slumped down, frustrated and disillusioned with his
career. He found out long ago that the only way that
he would get ahead at CubEx was to be an aggressive, bare-knuckled fighter, and Percy just wasn't that
kind of person. He was an excellent software engineer, so good that he was promoted five years ago to
Program Management, and that's when the unhap-
piness began. The job was constant role acting between a rock and a "hard place" and he rarely won.
He longed to get back to developing software again,
but knew that a backwards move in the company
would cost him his job grade. Worse yet, they were
bringing kids straight in from college using languag-
es that he didn't know. He knew that he was trapped.
And he was unhappy.

Knockknockknock came a quick rap on the door to
his office…"oh, now what?" Percy thought. "Yes, come
in!" Percy was surprised to see one of his younger
developers that he had taken a liking to, Vijay. He
was bright and didn't seem to carry the burden that

Percy did, and he was fun to be around. "Excuse me, Percy....do you have a minute?" asked Vijay. "Of course, have a seat!"

Percy was expecting Vijay to start asking him about the project that they were behind on, but instead Vijay started talking about investing and money, stunning Percy. "Have you heard about Options trading, Percy?" "Well, not much, but I hear that it's risky.... weren't those the trades that created the financial crisis in 2008?" Percy had done a little bit of stock trading and investing in the past, taking care of 401k allocations plus some small cash accounts on the side, but nothing serious. "Percy, I just went to this seminar last night where I learned about this trading program that teaches you about equity stock options. It's amazing! Did you know that you can create trades that generate income, and you don't even need to be right about the direction?" Percy thought about this for a minute....Vijay was not prone to jump on things that were not well-researched. Could it be true? "Sounds good, but what's the catch, Vijay?"

Vijay spent the next thirty minutes schooling Percy on a couple of simple strategies....Percy was hooked! Things were starting to look up...maybe there WAS a way out of his predicament. If he could put his money to work for HIM, perhaps he could fill those gaps and get ahead. The lift that Percy got from this newfound sense of optimism carried over to his overdue project, which he was able to finish that evening, far earlier than his wildest estimations. Vijay mentioned that the seminar would be repeated the next evening, so he cleared it with Jenna (she was somewhat puzzled but declined the invitation to accompany him) and made plans to attend.

What he saw at the seminar the next evening confirmed his optimism; the presenter was a bit "salesy" but every time they flashed an example up on the screen, Percy almost yelled out the answer in advance; he felt as if they were talking directly to HIM! During a break in the presentation, Percy called Jenna: "Honey, I'm at that presentation that I told you about….this is amazing! I think I'm going to sign up for their class….do you have any objections?" Jenna sounded somewhat distant and detached, offering: "Percy, if it's something that you want to do, then go ahead." Percy took that as a "yes" and plunked down his credit card at the next break, committing to a modest package that put him deeper in debt, but he felt as if his feet hardly touched the ground as he walked to his car that evening. He was going to learn to make money from the stock market! He could hardly wait to get started, and had trouble sleeping that evening.

From that moment on, Percy was like a man possessed; every waking moment was spent studying the charts and trading techniques. All sorts of new terms flew past his eyes, like "strike price" and "open interest." Percy and Vijay were inseparable at lunchtime, going over charts and strategies. And about six months later, Vijay dropped the bombshell: "Percy,

I'm going to turn in my two week notice. I'm going to trade for a living." Percy was both shocked and elated for Vijay; he hated to see him move on, but this is exactly what Percy wanted to accomplish! If Vijay could do it, maybe he could too. Vijay seemed to have a gift for it, and it didn't hurt that he had no mouths to feed at home, as he was still young and had little to lose.

But the other side of Percy's reaction came from the realization that Vijay seemed to do much better at this "trading" thing than Percy himself. Percy was stalled in his development.

At first it was pretty easy; he didn't think too hard about the trade and just kept everything very simple. He had some stunning wins out of the gate, to which Jenna smiled politely and said "that's nice, dear." But maybe she knew something, as every time he got some momentum, a bad trade would come along and knock him back to square one again….or worse. So, he decided to take a more measured approach, paper-trading a strategy successfully several times before he would put live capital behind it. As soon as he put live capital behind a trade, he would lose. His capital was now down below the starting point, and he didn't dare tell Jenna about this.

By now he was very "tuned in" to the various strategies and had started to follow several "gurus" beyond the initial company that he signed up for. Each one made their technique look SO EASY that he would follow along for a while, and as soon as he put live capital into a trade he would lose again! It might have been one trade in twenty that the guru would lose, but Percy somehow seemed to pick the ONE EXACT TRADE that was a loser. Percy was starting to get stressed out; not only was he distracted at work, watching the market constantly during the day while at his office, but also on his smartphone during lunch. His projects were starting to slide again and his VP was breathing down his neck again during staff meetings. Coincidentally, Vijay was reporting to him that he'd successfully made the transition to becoming

a profitable trader and was starting to attract trading capital from others. The pressure was starting
to boil inside of Percy; he took a walk at lunchtime
around the office grounds, staring at the positions on
his smartphone and cursing his luck, when he got an
idea. "I know….all of those successful traders….they
don't have to work in an office. They work from home,
and can FOCUS on their trades. That's my problem….
this Friday, I'll take a vacation day, trade from home
and make everything back that I've lost!" Percy could
barely contain his excitement at finding his "missing
link" and getting to Friday.

Friday saw him laying out his laptop and extra
screens on the kitchen table in the morning. Jenna
asked, "Percy, what are you doing? Aren't you going to the office?" "Not today, dear. I'm going to work
from home on this big project that I have." She gave
him an odd look before kissing him goodbye and
leaving for her job. As soon as she left, Percy wheeled
over the television and tuned into CNBC, and started
to listen to the banter….he rubbed his palms together
with excitement. He would be the tip of the spear
today….trading the same news as the professionals!
Today was his breakthrough day!

The trading day started with a quick win as Percy
scalped a futures contract trade for a couple of S&P500
points, netting him $100 on one contract. He was ec-
static, jumping up and slapping the ceiling. The family dog looked at him quizzically. Percy felt FREE for
the first time in years. At that moment, a breaking

news report came out on a stock he had been following, indicating an earnings pre-warning. This was going to be a slam-dunk; Percy immediately shorted the stock. He did it a little too quickly as he didn't calculate the margin required to hold short shares of that stock, just impulsively entering 400 shares because he felt that he needed to move quickly. Minutes later, he was dismayed to learn that he had next to no cash available for any additional trades; he'd have to sit with this one, but what the heck, this will be a great trade. The stock initially went lower on the news and Percy saw his account net rise by $500 - a six hundred dollar day so far! This was EASY and he started to mentally draft his resignation letter.

A chart alert brought him back to his senses; the stock was starting to RISE now. All of the earlier profits were gone in an instant and the stock started to squeeze higher in a dramatic fashion. "NOOOOOO!!!! What was going on?! "Percy yelled out. The dog went down in the basement to hide…..his daily P/L was dropping….now down -$1000 and dropping by the minute. A foreign sound interrupted his panic….the telephone. Was it the office? He picked up the phone and answered…."Mr. Hedger? This is Andrew from your broker CheaperTrade….you have insufficient funds to maintain your current position. We are requesting that you liquidate your position or we will do it for you." A MARGIN CALL!!! Oh. My. God. Percy mumbled to Andrew to just close the position. A quick check on his statement showed that he was now down over $3000 on the day, about 10% of his account. Percy was beside himself….his mind was spinning. He noticed that the S&P chart was moving higher on the 5 minute chart and made a snap judgement that if he traded 10 contracts of futures long, he could get that $3k back with a 6 point move. He went "long" those ten contracts, and that instant marked the exact high water mark for the day, as the chart began to reverse immediately. Within 5 minutes it was DOWN six points, equaling his earlier loss.

The phone rang once more; Andrew again. A blur. Screaming, screaming, mind spinning, rage and betrayal. Pressure building up beyond the ability to control. He balled up his fist and knocked it straight through the kitchen wall, opening a hole to the garage. There was no pain, only a mindless rage that screaming did not seem to abate. Grabbing the laptop and heading outside, he watched with detached amusement that the laptop seemed to be almost aerodynamic as it spun in a long, graceful arc towards the ground, 20 yards from where Percy threw it. The shattering of the laptop against the driveway seemed to startle Percy, as he slowly became aware of his surroundings and his predicament. He had just lost over six thousand dollars in only minutes, (not counting the laptop) and he struggled to understand how and why it had happened.

Slowly his composure returned, and the self-loathing returned with it. "Man, I must be the WORST trader on the planet. How could I DO that?!" Not only was he minus one laptop and six thousand dollars, but now he had a hole in the wall that he was going to have to fix pronto. He quickly buzzed out to the home store to get some patching materials; if he was quick about it, he'd have it patched and painted before Jenna returned this evening from her job. He could deal with the loss of $6k but not the disappointment from her.

Fortunately, Percy was a fairly handy guy and the initial patch & joint compound went on fairly quickly to both sides of the wall, so he left it to dry. As Percy scoured the garage for the matching paint, he suddenly felt a very heavy fatigue set in. He noticed he was still very tense and clenching his jaw, so while the "mud" dried, he felt it would be ok to slump down on the couch for a minute and close his eyes. He fell into an instant sleep....

He awoke to a strange sound, startled....and strained his eyes to see something that was in the room with him. "What.....who is there!?" He sat up and could just barely make out the image of....something familiar....."Percy, I am your Father." A shiver went down Percy's spine as he recognized the voice of his deceased father, ten years gone. It was a shimmering image, transparent, yet with defined features....like a ghost that you'd see in a bad movie. Was this really happening to him? His Father continued, "Do you believe your eyes that it is me?" Percy's voice had gone dry, as he only managed a dry squeak, "Yes, Dad." There were so many things that he wanted to ask him, but the apparition continued: "You will be visited by three spirits; tonight the first, and every night at midnight thereafter until complete. Heed their words, my son." And then he was gone, drifting away into the light of the afternoon. Percy's pulse was racing, he wasn't sure if what he had just seen was a dream or was real.

Just then the door opened, and Jenna walked in. "Hi honey, how was your day?" Percy's mind raced as he tried to compose a response. "Ok, I guess..." was all that he could manage. Jenna shot him a quizzical look and then started reviewing her day and her troubling patients, but Percy's mind was elsewhere. What happened today? The whole day seemed surreal, as if he lived it through someone else's eyes, and then that THING with his Dad? But what was gnawing at this stomach was his absolute failure as a trader today. "Percy…..Percy……PERCY honey what happened to the wall here?" asked Jenna. Oh damn, THAT. "Oh, I spilled some water on the floor and slipped. My arm went right through the wall." You could see Jenna mentally calculating what it would look like to see someone slipping on water, and arresting their fall by punching their arm through the wall. "Are you OK? Percy? You don't look like yourself. Are you still OK to go to the Walkers' tonight?" Oh. That. Percy had also forgotten about their dinner party for that evening. He knew that he needed to get hold of his sanity soon.

At the dinner party, Percy kept reviewing what his Father had said about being visited by spirits for the next three nights. The Walkers were good friends, and after a couple of beers he started to relax and laugh again. That whole "ghost" thing with his Father must have been a dream, he decided. Percy and Jenna eventually left the party and like most evenings, Percy read a trading strategy book until his eyes would no longer stay open, and he drifted off into a troubled sleep.

# Chapter Two:
# Past, Present, and Future

"Who's there!" cried Percy as he awoke, startled, his heart racing. A noise.... yet like nothing that he had heard before. It was more of a.....presence that he felt. He looked at the clock in the blackness of his room - midnight. Was that vision of his father yesterday just a dream? Yet just as he warned, there was....something there with him. A soft light which he barely noticed at first, started to intensify as it came nearer to him, and then suddenly took the shape of a face. A child....or was it an old man? "Are you the one my father warned me of?" asked Percy.

"Yes. " Said the Spirit…."Take my hand and come with me." Percy shook his head and tried to clear the fog…."But who are you? Where are we going?"

"I am the ghost of Trading Past. I wish to show you what once was. "

Percy took the hand of the spirit and experienced movement without moving…hovering without any sense of gravity. They were instantly transported to a place where he recognized, which was his first Options seminar. Percy could see himself sitting in his seat. "That's me!" he shouted; the ghost said nothing. Percy focused on his former self and instantly connected with the feeling of promise, and the hope and expectations of what this new form of opportunity was going to give him. He got a chill up his spine just reliving those memories, and it felt GOOD to feel that sense of optimism again.

The ghost interrupted, "Do you remember this way?" Percy nodded. "Then let us be gone." The ghost tugged again and suddenly they were moving without any sense of flight.

When they stopped, Percy did not recognize the next place at first. There was a young man working behind a set of screens, quietly and patiently studying the patterns…..it was Vijay!

"Vijay!" Percy shouted…"it's Percy!" The Ghost of Trading Past eased up to Percy and said, "He cannot hear you, we are in the past. Observe."

Percy watched Vijay, literally over his shoulder. Vijay studied the charts and talked to himself quietly, walking through the steps of the trade before he entered. Percy could not be certain, but from the looks of the chart it appeared to him that Vijay just got "stopped out" and took a loss within about a minute of his entry. Yet Vijay was quiet, passive, and unemotional. Vijay wrote some notes in a logbook and went back at it, and Percy watched as Vijay then ripped off a trade that earned double the amount of the losing trade just ten minutes earlier. Yet there was no reaction from Vijay. He was just as quiet and passive, noting the results in his logbook.

And as suddenly as it had happened, the ghost was gone and Percy was back in his bed. He looked over at Jenna, who was still sleeping soundly. Percy's mind raced as he tried to make sense of what he had just seen. He saw himself in his seminar, and recognized that sense of optimism and awe which had disappeared some time ago as he struggled to stay positive with his trading, not to mention Friday's disaster. And what about Vijay? How fascinating was it to watch someone so talented, yet impassive....quietly go about his business?

Percy's mind then went back to his father's earlier warning, *"You will be visited by three spirits; tonight the first, and every night at midnight thereafter...."* He wondered what tomorrow night would bring. Did he just dream all of this? Or did it really happen to him? He closed his eyes and replayed the events in his mind, and before long Percy was asleep again.

Percy woke the next morning, made small talk with Jenna and then got to his weekend errands, the first of which was painting over his patch. Yet he still couldn't shake the experiences of the last 24 hours.... first seeing a vision of his father, and then some ghost claiming to be from "trading past." He clearly got the message of that experience, recapturing the optimism and possibility. But he still wasn't sure if the whole experience was a dream or if it was real. Regardless, the sense of awareness did not go away. He *had* lost that sense of optimism that so captured him early on.

"Yeah"...Percy said to himself, "It was all so easy back then."

The day flew by, but his experience had not escaped the eagle eye of Jenna. "Are you OK?" she asked. "You seem sort of preoccupied." "Guilty" thought Percy.

"No honey I just have a big report due on Monday and I've been thinking of ways to tackle it."

Jenna shot him a sideways look, shrugged and walked away. Did she know what happened last night? The evening came all too quickly, and Percy went to bed with a sense of trepidation and excitement….would it happen again tonight? Percy slipped into an uneasy sleep before he was once again startled by a noise in the dark room.

This time the experience was a little more immediate, as a somewhat rough-looking soul appeared right in Percy's face and growled, "Right, let's go. C'mon." Percy obeyed by grabbing his hand, and once again they were transported without any sense of movement. "Wh…who are you?" asked Percy.

"I am the ghost of trading present. I will show you what is."

Once they stopped moving, Percy immediately recognized the next location as his own house. In fact, it was YESTERDAY, right back to the scene of the crime. He recognized everything happening, but it was very different watching it from a third person perspective. Percy's immediate thought as he saw the whole trading day unravel was….what an IDIOT! Why did he allow himself to get so worked up over little things? And his "revenge trading" was ugly to watch, and made him look away. The scruffy ghost looked at him and said, "Do you see what is?" Percy nodded, "Yes, yes I do." "Then let us be off."

They flew to a familiar location, Vijay's place again. It was the same as before, although Vijay had significantly upgraded his equipment. But watching him win and lose was EXACTLY as it was before. There was no reaction; there was no panic on the losses nor elation on the wins. Just quiet.....execution. And just as suddenly as before, Percy was back in bed, left to contemplate the visions that he had just seen. It took some time to get back to sleep, because he was starting to become very aware of the differences in approach between himself and Vijay. His young friend was just a very passive machine processing the information and applying it to the charts. Percy began to realize how erratic that his own approach was, and how it lacked in structure and edge. Once again the spirit interrupted him, "Do you see what is?" Percy nodded again, and without delay Percy was deposited back into his bed to contemplate what he just saw. Now he was sure that this was actually happening to him, and that it was no longer a dream. "But why me? What are they trying to tell me?" thought Percy.

Sunday flew by without pause, and once more Percy found himself going to bed, feeling uneasy about what might happen at midnight. This one was to be the third and final visit....what would this one entail. Percy watched the clock for some time before suddenly sensing someone else in the room, roll-

ing in on a form of scooter. Percy was startled when a very odd, angular figure got in his face and spoke with a stentorian tone, "I am the ghost of the trading future. I will show you the shadows of things that have not happened, but might happen in the time before us. The future has not been set." Percy was left to ponder the weight of that statement as he grabbed the spirit's hand and was whisked away.

The next scene was one that Percy was very familiar with....his own house, from the outside. He seemed to be hovering in the air, looking down from above. Jenna was packing the family van....with all of her clothes, as well as that of their children. Jenna was upset and was moving with a rough purpose. Their kids were hanging around the van, looking very stiff and awkward, with his daughter crying. Percy watched himself come out of the house and argue with Jenna while the kids just quietly got into the van. Percy could not hear the conversation, but it was not necessary as it was easy to read their body language. The reality of it hit Percy between the eyes.... one possible future was him losing his family, as it was clear that they were leaving him.

The ghost stared at him for a minute and saw that the message had sunk in. "Come...." Said the spirit....and they flew to the next location, which was his office at CubEx. Once again, he was viewing a conversation from above, this time it was the Division VP talking with the head of Human Resources. "We can't explain it, "said the VP, "he was a good employee for years, very dependable. And then suddenly he was gone. He was here, but he was not here if you know what I mean. Unproductive and argumentative. It was unfortunate, but we had to let him go last week. I don't know if it was drugs or booze or something else. The poor guy just snapped like a twig. He'll have a few weeks of unemployment, but it'll be hard for him to find something at his age." The head of HR nodded in agreement, signed a few papers and shoved them across the desk to the Division VP, who took them and left. Just like that, Percy was an unemployed 50 year-old.

Percy watched from above, shocked. He was cold as ice. "My family, my job....what else can they take from me?!" The ghost said nothing, just pointing at Percy. "I don't want this to happen!" The ghost ignored him and maintained his pose, pointing at Percy. "Take me away from here!" Percy yelled. The ghost ignored him and continued to point. Percy's vision began to blur as he felt himself spinning into blackness.....

## Chapter Three:
# A Second Chance

Percy slowly opened his eyes, looking around at his bedroom. Light was beginning to filter in from the window, and the sound of chirping birds caught his attention. "My family!" he thought… ."Are they still here?" A quick look next to him in the bed showed that Jenna was still there, purring quietly as she slept. A huge sense of relief washed over Percy; he felt as if he had leaned fully over the precipice, yet caught himself before he tumbled. With this relief came a renewed sense of purpose and motivation…that version of the future was NOT going to happen to him!

He did a quick replay of what he had experienced over the weekend:

- A meltdown and huge losses on Friday.

- A visit from his father, warning him of the subsequent visits

- A visit from the ghost of trading past, reminding him of the optimism and promise of what he wanted.

- A visit from the ghost of trading present, showing him not only his own failure, but of Vijay's continued success.

- A visit from the ghost of trading future, showing him one possible future where he lost everything.

A future that he did not want to be part of. One that he was going to change, starting right now. "Jenna!" he nudged his wife..."Let's go get some breakfast!" She stirred and yawned....

"Mmmmm? But Percy....it's 6am on Monday! Don't you have to work today?"

"Yes, but it can wait. I have a lot to talk to you about!"

Percy and Jenna quickly got dressed and drove out to a little diner on the edge of town, where Percy proceeded to tell her about the events over his weekend. At first, she was a bit wide-eyed, then began to relax and nodded along with Percy's story. When Percy wrapped up the story, Jenna said: "Percy honey, I know that this means the world to you, and it could mean something special for us down the road when you get this to work for you. I don't know if what you experienced was real or a dream, but I just want you to know that I'm here to help, not to judge. Don't feel stress on my behalf to shortcut the path to success. Do what you have to do to make this work. How can I help?"

Percy was so excited he could hardly sit still; for a man who had lost it all over the course of a weekend, he suddenly realized how fortunate that he was to get a second chance in life, and he wasn't going to mess it up this time. He returned to work that day with a new spring in his step, and the day was more effortless than he imagined that it would be. The job was suddenly fun again, but as he began to think of his trading career, he realized that the excitement was back, and he would get back to work that evening. But first, a phone call to finish the day. "Hello Vijay, this is Percy. I was wondering if you'd have any time to meet up for coffee this week......."

Yes, if you're wondering, I adopted this fictional story from Charles Dickens' "A Christmas Carol" as it so elegantly shows what a person can learn from past and present experiences, and how they can shape their future with that awareness. And being one degree off on your initial departure bearing can mean being hundreds of miles off course if your destination is thousands of miles away. This is where "course corrections" come into play, and is why I placed this story at the front end of this book.


## Did You Recognize Yourself?

I wrote the story about Percy Hedger because his story is what the average trader goes through in their progression to "make it" in this business. And if you're at all human, then you've probably recognized at least a few behaviors along the way that you might be sharing with Percy. Let's catalog some of these:

- One of the things that you see adding stress to Percy's situation is that he's trying to create this utopian version of his success to Jenna, his wife. If that's not currently true, as in Percy's case, then this just creates more internal tension and performance anxiety to create approval.

- Percy displayed one of the most common traits of newer traders, which is trading upon "known" information. Trading professionals have already discounted it hours or days ago, and are taking the opposite side of that trade.

- Percy had certain "expectations" of the stocks/markets that he was following; like many investors who find their way into this business, they expect a linear cause & effect relationship between news/results, and the price. Most are usually shocked to discover that the market or individual stock prices do not "correctly" respond to standard linear logic. Price movement quite often does not make "sense" and it can be disconcerting to those whose current career has been based upon unbreakable models, such as Accounting or Engineering.

- Percy was a very emotional trader. Who wouldn't get emotional if you had lost a big percentage of your account in only minutes? Percy needed to find a way to disconnect the trading results from his emotions, like Vijay had. He'll soon find that there are very simple ways to accomplish this.

- Percy was "revenge trading." This is a form of "oh yeah, you're going to stop me out for a loss? I'll show YOU who's boss!" If you've never experienced this form of personal hell, it almost never works out well. The Market is always right, no matter what we think of its rationale.

- Percy did not have a structured approach to the market. His approach was more like many newer investors would be like if they went to a casino...."Hey, let's try a round of blackjack, and then I'll play some Roulette, and then try my luck at the one-armed bandits!" A jack of all trades is a master of none.

- Finally, Percy was being delusional with the one true sympathetic friend that he had - himself. Many newer investors have to learn the hard way that the Market is extraordinarily unforgiving and does not give second chances...there are no "mulligans" when you are trading against the best in the world. And learning to be honest with yourself and critical of your own performance - without becoming self-deprecating - is key to survival.

## Chapter Four:
# The Two Minds

Of all the billions of dollars that is spent on science every year, researching and understanding things like how frogs communicate, how dolphins speak, how bears hibernate, etc....one of the true mysteries of our time is *still* the Human Mind. Why do we do what we do? Why do we act in the way that we do? And more specifically, why do some people "think" their way to a fortune while others appear to be stuck in the mud, suffering the same "bad luck" again and again? It turns out that there is actual science behind these actions and decisions, using knowledge that we're only just beginning to understand.

Stay with me on this, because before long, you'll start to see WHY this science is so crucial to your future success, and WHAT we can do about it right now!

## The Holy Grail of Trading

If you've spent any time around this activity that we call "trading", you'll see the same insatiable drive towards what is commonly known as the "Holy Grail" of trading strategies. What is it? Well, what we're all after....that mythical strategy that risks no capital while producing outstanding returns again and again, without losses. Wouldn't that be great? Just log into our broker's account every day and watch the balance perpetually grow.

But somehow it never seems to happen to us; we see all of these great strategies and programs and they look so simple, so easy....like catching fish in a trout pond with a net. But when we go to apply that strategy, we find out that it's NOT that simple, that losses are REAL, and we become disillusioned with that strategy, and resume our hunt for the Grail.

Would it surprise you for me to state that I have FOUND that Holy Grail of trading? You already have it right now, but I need to first show you how to unlock it in these next couple of chapters....by first showing you how your mind....or as we'll see, *minds*.... operates.

## My Journey into Neuroscience

My path has been no different than any other retail investor hoping to earn their future in the financial markets. As we'll soon see, there is a "progression" that everyone goes through, without exception, to "earn the right" to become a professional investor trading the markets. It's the very rare bird that becomes a "Turtle Trader" and is financially successful overnight just by following a recipe. What I'm getting at here is that I've been in your shoes before, as has every trader that now makes their living from the financial markets.

And I have to give credit for this journey into neuroscience to one of my first mentors. This individual was not a particularly good trader, as he was very impulsive. He belonged in front of a crowd. But once I got to know this individual, he had me studying all sorts of self-help authors and their material. The usual suspects were devoured, such as Brian Tracy, Zig Ziglar, Jim Rohn, and Tony Robbins. I had studied these individuals in the past but quickly got discouraged, because my thought at the time was, "How am I supposed to use this material at my oppressive corporate job?" So when I started to study investing, suddenly I saw an application for these materials. And they were fun, and allowed me to expand my definition of success, which was admittedly very narrow when I began this journey.

If I could sum up the lessons from these materials, it was messages such as "You have great potential! Get organized! Look on the bright side! Be positive in everything that you do!" and so on. I would listen to them over and over again much to the distress of my family, who were frankly getting tired of hearing Tony snap his fingers and tell stories in an enthusiastic tone whenever we took a family trip. I had plateaued on self-help motivational materials. There's no doubt that they had helped me immensely in looking at my life from a new perspective, without which I never would have abandoned my former corporate life. But I needed something different at this point.

And then an interesting connection occurred; someone asked me, "Have you seen *The Secret*?" I had not, nor had I heard about it. I got an earful from an enthusiastic student, and I invested in the DVD.

When I watched it for the first time, I was floored. Suddenly, all of the "good things" that had happened to me were explained. I began to go further down the rabbit hole, by researching and investing in the various authors that contributed to The Secret movie. And that has led me deeper and deeper down this path of "Neuroscience" to the point that I'm at least conversant in it, while not claiming to be an expert. And I INSTANTLY saw the connection to trading performance, and have been incorporating it into all of the materials that I teach in the OptionsMD program. I believe that Neuroscience is the "missing link" when it comes to investing success, and you simply cannot operate without it.

So then, let me start with the first law of Neuroscience that I learned, which is the **Law of Attraction**.

## The Law of Attraction

The Law of Attraction is fairly simple; you will *attract* everything that comes into your life, good and bad. Ever knew a lucky friend that just seemed to have everything go their way no matter what? Or a friend who was a "human Eeyore" that always had something wrong happening to them, either with health or circumstance. Yep, this is the "Law of Attraction" at work. For now, let's not peek under the covers to figure out WHY this is happening, I just need you to accept that **you will attract everything that comes into your life**.

Now, when most investors find out about something like this, they put it to work in the wrong way. They read up about the Law of Attraction, and spend a couple of minutes in thought:

"I want all my debt to go away! No more debt!"

Guess what they attract more of in their lives? **DEBT**.

The way that the Law of Attraction works….**you will "manifest" what you focus on**. Napoleon Hill put it best in his fabulous book "Think and Grow Rich"….. "Thoughts Become Things." Those three words are very powerful and I want you to keep that phrase in mind as we move forward….."Thoughts" truly do become "Things" as you'll see. In this example, what was this person focusing their thoughts on? Debt. What did they receive more of? Debt.

Now compare that example with this one....let's say that the same person wanted more abundance in their lives, and focused on receiving an extra $100 in income every week.

They built visual images of what it would feel like to receive that extra $100....they imagined their bank balance $100 higher....they could *see* the check being handed to them....they focused on the methods that they were going to use to create that extra $100 of income....they mentally created the experience, one step shy of actually experiencing it.

Is it then any wonder that they usually manifest that $100...or more...from that point forward?

I experienced this effect without understanding it.... months before I first quit my job to become a full-time trader. I created a mental inventory of what date that I would turn in my notice, who I would give it to, what that notice would say, what my bank balance would look like the day that I quit, what my home office would look like.....EVERYTHING. I had mentally created this scenario so many times in my head, all with the same outcome, that it almost became a "deja vu" moment when it finally occurred. I had done all of the right things to attract that outcome.

Now imagine if my mindset in the month or two before I had planned to quit.....was instead: "Oh man, I hope I don't screw this up! I just *know* that there's going to be some funky move coming up in the market that's going to spoil my move. I'd better tread carefully so I'm prepared for that bad move…."

I think you can see by now that I would have attracted some piece of "bad luck" that would have stalled my progress. And chances are, I'd *still* be working there, chained to my desk.

Thoughts become Things, so you need to very carefully monitor your thoughts so that you're manifesting what you want, and not more of what you don't want.

OK, so the "Law of Attraction" is fun, but very "fluffy" in a way that has a lot of folks "harrumph'ing" and looking for the science behind it. Investors are a pragmatic bunch and are not taken in by puffery. So what, then, is the science behind the Law of Attraction and what makes it work?

## The Two Different Minds

Have you ever had a completely mystifying experience making a trade, as if you yourself did not make the trade? The *"how could I have been so stupid"* kind of trade? The one that leaves you shaking your head and wondering just what you did?

Well, you're not alone and there's a very specific reason why it happens. The part of you that thinks that it's in control…..*is really not in control*. It's because of the two different minds that you have, and you haven't learned to use them just yet.

Most of you have heard of "Left-Brained" vs. "Right-Brained" people. The left-brained are the accountants and clerks of the world, the right-brained are the artists and musicians of the world. Each side looks at the other like they're a little odd, and the rest of us are somewhat in the middle between being analytical and abstract.

But what we're talking about here is completely different....you have both a **Conscious Mind** and a **Subconscious Mind** working in tandem.

The Conscious Mind is task-oriented and requires you to actually devote thought towards the task at hand. The Subconscious mind, however, does everything in the background, automatically, and without effort. And it never....ever....stops.

You can think of the Subconscious Mind as the "inner core" of your brain, chugging along in the background, quietly handling the millions of things that happen every second to run the biochemistry in your body as well as the other complex reasoning functions that we typically associate with "intuition"..... while the Conscious Mind is the "outer core" that everything must pass through. For reasons that we'll soon see, the Subconscious mind is many orders of magnitude more powerful than the Conscious mind.

Let's discuss a couple of examples so you can quickly see the difference between the two. Remember when you learned how to drive? Hands at "ten" and "two" on the steering wheel, sitting up straight, you were acutely aware of every action that was required to drive the car. You had to *consciously* think about every action that you took, whether it was shifting the car into gear, figuring out the turn signal stalk, or where to place your foot to hit the brakes. Your **Conscious Mind** was doing all the work.

Think about this: when you last drove your car, did you THINK about anything at all? No, you just put the key in, started up the car, and then the next thing you knew, you were at your destination. Your Conscious Mind did very little of the work, only relaying various data points like traffic signals and whether or not it's raining and the wipers need to be turned on. The Subconscious mind did all of the work. In fact, this is a natural progression because the Conscious Mind loses focus every six to ten seconds, while the Subconscious Mind NEVER loses focus.

Another example might be a golf swing. When you first learn to play golf you have hundreds of "swing thoughts" coursing through your Conscious mind, like "keep your left arm straight" and "don't look up", followed a few years later by "swing from the inside - out" and "don't reverse pivot." After you've spent a few thousand hours hitting golf balls, it becomes "automatic", which is just code for the fact that the Subconscious mind is now running your swing.

Of course, what happens if you stand over a crucial, pressure-packed shot? Your Conscious mind tries to take control again and completely flubs it, because you simply can't "think" your way through a golf shot.

And what about a crucial free-throw in a championship basketball game? If you see a player "think" their way through a free throw then you'll surely see some heavy masonry as the ball clanks off the rim for a "miss." Only if the player allows his inner "core," or Subconscious mind to visualize the shot and simply let it happen will you see the player swish that shot.

We constantly see examples of athletes who make silly mistakes as rookies or Freshmen.....yet they become smooth and natural with experience, as they constantly relate how the game has "slowed down" for them and allows them to make plays with ease, where they were too busy "thinking" when they were less experienced.

Example after example...the Conscious Mind is a clumsy oaf, yet very good at sorting through information and being objective. It has no doubt that the traffic light is red, or what time it is when it looks at a watch. And it serves as the eyes and ears for the powerful core processor, the Subconscious mind.

So really, what we're saying is that **the Subconscious Mind is really in charge**. In fact, the Conscious Mind is only responsible for controlling between

2 to 4 percent of our actions! [v]We can "think" that we're in charge of our lives through sheer will, but any effects will be temporary until we tap into the power of the Subconscious Mind. Ever try to stick to a diet through sheer willpower alone? Quit smoking? Didn't work, did it? You couldn't explain to anyone else why you failed, you just did. No change is lasting unless it comes from within, the Subconscious Mind.

Those who have not yet learned to harness the strengths - and liabilities - of the Subconscious mind are forever enslaved by their mysterious ability *to do exactly the wrong thing at the right time*. There is nothing more frustrating in the trading world and it forces the majority that cannot solve this puzzle....to quit. Now, let's forget about that option as a possibility and see what we have to do to let our minds do the right thing.

## The RAS, or Reticular Activating System

OK, we've talked about the two "minds" so far; how are they connected together? Well, this is where things get interesting. The "RAS" is a network of nerves that connects signals from the various parts of your brain and spinal cord, and acts as a "filter" to your brain from all of the external senses like sight, smell, touch, and hearing. [vi]You can think of this RAS as a "gate-keeper" that looks for specific inputs and funnels them instantly to your brain. Ever notice how you can hear your own name even in a loud, crowded room? That's the RAS doing its job. See your kids instantly across a crowded room? That's the RAS again.

Have you ever noticed that when you pick up a new interest, all of a sudden you see it everywhere? When I first got interested in motorcycles, I mean SERIOUS-LY interested in them, then I began to see them EV-ERYWHERE, day and night. It's not that they weren't there before….they were….it's just that my RAS was not instructed to "look" for them.

And THIS is why the RAS is hugely important, and ties into that statement that I wrote earlier, that "Thoughts Become Things." When you tell your RAS what you are looking for, it will search Heaven and Earth to find it. And find it, it will. This is why it is so important to NOT program your goals around what you DON'T WANT, but rather only those things that you DO want.

And this is why author John Assaraf says that "Worry is a prayer for what you don't want." Think about all of the time and energy that you've spent worrying about things that were out of your control, yet it seemed like the more that you worried about the possibility of something negative happening, the more likely that it was to occur.

So how does our mind tell this RAS "gatekeeper" what to focus on?

## Learning New Behaviors and Reaching Goals

Here is the "good news/bad news" thing when it comes to learning new behaviors: **All we have to do is to "program" the Subconscious Mind into "accepting" the behaviors that we want from the RAS.** The Subconscious Mind tells the RAS what it wants to do, and the RAS spends 24 hours a day looking for those inputs that match up with the desired behavior. If you program it that you want to avoid debt, then it will tell the RAS to go find everything that it can about debt, usually leading to activities that increase debt. Remember, your Conscious mind only controls 2-4% of your activities, so it has very little influence on achieving goals.

You've heard the advice that "people who write down their goals will achieve them." In a recent study, it was shown that only 3% of the participants had written goals (vs. 13% with unwritten goals and 84% with no goals) were earning 10 times as much as the other 97% combined.[vii] Those 3% of "goal-writers" were unconsciously training their Subconscious Minds to allow their RAS to filter valuable information to enable them to reach their goals.

Learning new behaviors and reaching your goals is a relatively simple process then, although it's not "easy" at first. You have to teach your Subconscious Mind what it wants. You have to "train" your mind to seek out and find information that is congruent with your goals and desires, taking care to focus on the CORRECT things.

And here's more good news; the Subconscious Mind accepts whatever the RAS allows as input. And it does not have to be real. Ever notice how powerful a dream can be? It's not real, yet your mind didn't know the difference. How long did it take you to "come back to reality" after you woke up? You can "input" images into your Subconscious mind simply by closing your eyes and visualizing them. In fact, this form of Neuroscience has already been proven to be very effective in the sports psychology world; you can see athletes closing their eyes and mentally "going through the motions" in preparation for their event, regardless of whether it's downhill skiing, gymnastics, platform diving, or a soccer free kick. I recently watched pro golfer Jason Day win the PGA Championship; before every shot he would take the time to close his eyes and "visualize" the shot that he was about to take. Mentally "programming" your mind through live or imaginary images leads to that "law of attraction" in being able to manifest what it is that we want. In Jason's case, it was the Wanamaker trophy.

The Subconscious Mind also does not question the input supplied to it, IF it is able to get past the Gate-keeper. This is where it's so important to focus on what we want without judgement, (What! You'll never be able to make that much money in a month! You can't time the Market! 95% fail at trading!.....

etc....) so that we can correctly "train" the Subconscious Mind into telling the RAS what it wants it to seek for. In some cases this has been so effective that criminals become convinced that they did not commit the crime that they did, simply because they've very effectively communicated information past the RAS and into the Subconscious mind.

## Your Financial Blueprint

The more that I understood about Neuroscience, the Law of Attraction kept putting me in the path of more valuable information relating to the pursuit of Investing. And one of the new concepts for me was about the "Financial Blueprint" that everyone has, and how it was controlling my income. I read "Secrets of the Millionaire Mind" by T. Harv Eker which is just a different, but consistent adaptation/explanation of how the brain works.

His theory about the Financial Blueprint is this:

- If you believe that $100,000 is what you should be earning, then your Subconscious Mind will ensure that you attain that level of success - and no more. If you receive a sudden windfall, your Subconscious Mind will sabotage your trading efforts until your income level drops back to where your Subconscious Mind says that it should be.

- If you believe that only "bad" people are rich, or that earning trading profits takes money away from others and that's a "bad thing", then your Subconscious Mind will find a way to surreptitiously surrender those winnings back to the Market.

- If you see your winnings approaching a round number (such as $10,000 or $100,000) and you can't believe that you've done that well....and wonder if you deserve it....then your Subconscious Mind will find a way for you NOT to exceed those round number levels.

Think about this for a second....how many Lottery winners are destitute and broke, only a year or two after winning millions of dollars? I mean, that person should be set for LIFE with that amount of income, but inside their Subconscious Mind, their "Financial Blueprint" is in direct conflict with the winnings, and the constant internal battle of "I don't deserve this" will ALWAYS defeat them.

Hopefully by this point you're having an "a-ha!" moment or at least a "yeah, no kidding" response. Most traders will go on for years without understanding that there are actually much deeper forces at work, inside of THEM, that directly govern their financial success. This is why those traders who have achieved a "Mastery" level are so calm, so placid. They know that it's not the MARKET that they're fighting....the true battle is one waged WITHIN every trader, and they've won that battle.

And the more experiences that you've had in your life, the greater the "catalog" of responses that the Subconscious mind has to judge your activities and make appropriate corrective actions. Think about it, your Subconscious Mind doesn't consult you about the decisions that it makes about your blood sugar, pulse rate, sleep schedule, digestion, cell regrowth, or any of the millions of decisions that it makes on the fly. Why should it give you any insight as to how it will govern your trading decisions?

## Training the Subconscious Mind

OK, now that we've explored WHY our minds act in the way that we do, what are we going to do about it? Why, we're going to train that Subconscious Mind to give us what we want, of course. Let's do that next….

# Chapter Five:
# Creating the Trader's Mindset

O K, let's do a quick reset; I threw a lot of new information at you in the last chapter, which is very likely where readers will pause and put the book down because it didn't align with their current belief structure. It's time to move past the theory and into the practical world of application so that we can learn to be consistently profitable investors, but to do so we need to "hack" the mind to create the performance that we want. Let's summarize where we were, so that we can then start to focus on adapting the mind to trading. In the last chapter:

- We saw that there are essentially two "minds", the "Conscious" and the "Subconscious" mind.

- These two minds have different roles from an operating and learning perspective.

- The Subconscious Mind is really in charge and makes the vast majority of decisions, although we "see" the world through the Conscious Mind. We think that we can "control" our actions through the Conscious Mind but rarely does this generate lasting results.

• Your Subconscious Mind has a very specific "Belief System" that it operates by; this Belief System is the set of rules that you live by and has been built up your entire life.

• The Subconscious Mind instructs the Reticular Activating System, or "RAS" to seek out and find information that is CONSISTENT with that belief system.

• If our belief system is such that we firmly believe that we should profit from market activities, then the RAS will find information consistent with supporting that performance. Conversely, if our Subconscious Mind does NOT believe that we can or should profit from market activities, then it will instruct the RAS to seek out information consistent with creating poor performance.

It should be clear by reading these summary bullets that our current Belief System is really the key to whether we succeed or fail at investing in the market; let's understand what this Belief System is, and how to set it up for success in the markets....

## Understanding our Belief System

As we grow from children to adults, we build experience and add "layers" to our lives. By doing so we build a Belief System that defines who we are. And our Subconscious mind tells our RAS to go out and find things that agree with our current set of beliefs. Some would come to the conclusion that the older that you are, the less "adaptive" that you are to learning new concepts. And we see evidence of this every day:

- People tuning into the "version" of news that aligns with their current belief structure.

- Those that are only able to listen to a musical genre that's consistent with their belief structure, what they consider to be "good music."

- Investors that are surprised/disappointed by a move in the markets that goes against what they believe, or their "bias."

And I work with investing students every day that are unable to quickly grasp new concepts....because they conflict with ones that they have adopted much earlier in their trading development, usually from questionable (yet powerful) sources such as TV commercials. Once these concepts become "imprinted" into your belief structure, they are literally impossible to act against.

As we've shown, I firmly believe that this is just a "state of mind", that anyone at any age can learn whatever they want, or that they can adopt new behaviors....including new beliefs and habits required to be "in sync" with the Market. What it comes down to is the MOTIVATION that you need to be able to grow and change. (We'll cover this important aspect shortly!)

What we'll do in this chapter, then, is to discuss *how we can change that Belief System* into something more wealth-and-success-positive, so that we can learn to embrace behaviors and activities that create the results that fit our goals. Put more directly, as we build these skills we'll learn how to make (and keep) more money. The first thing that we need to do, however, is understand that the Belief System that many of us come into the world of Investing with….is preventing us from making money.

## We Are Wired Incorrectly to Trade

What do I mean by this statement? Through our adult lives and through our careers, the Subconscious Mind becomes an effective "risk manager" for us. We learn that when we touch a hot stove, we get burned….and we also learn that when we take on a project with too much risk at work, we can also get burned, so our Conscious Mind takes over. Whenever anything looks "dicey" the Subconscious mind steps in and puts out the fire, based on what we usually call "instinct." We also refer to this as "the little voice in the back of our head" or we sometimes attribute this to "a hunch" or "intuition." Most of us are familiar with this concept of "intuitive decisions" but few of us are familiar with where they come from, nor how they influence us daily.

When we start to trade, we're usually not very effective risk managers. Trading is still "fun" at this point as we associate trading with pleasure. But before long, the Subconscious Mind will start to step in with a negative influence as our first trade begins to fall into the "red" and take some heat. Chances are good that this position is using far too much capital and we're starting to lose sleep worrying about it; unfortunately, this is a "rite of passage" for every trader when first starting out. The Subconscious Mind begins to bargain with you…."I know that you're feeling pain, and I can take it away for you. I really think that you should let me control the risk on this position and close it down."

(Imagine this line being spoken with the voice of the HAL 9000 computer from the movie "2001: A Space Odyssey" and you'll perfectly understand how soothing that the Subconscious Mind can be)

Typically this action is OUTSIDE of our rule set, so if you've ever made an impulsive trading decision which is not listed in your rule set, this is precisely what you'll see. So no, you're not a "bad trader" or anything like that, you just haven't trained your Subconscious Mind properly yet. As we'll see in subsequent chapters, there are various stages that an investor goes through, or a "progression" of stages where you incrementally acquire skill. In the early stages, before you've begun to master your "Mindset", the Subconscious Mind will instruct you to start looking for "safety." This is an absolutely natural and linear response to risk, isn't it? It's one that we've done through our whole lives…. when faced with danger, either "fight" or "take flight."

Unfortunately this flight to "safe harbor" usually means that you're allowing your Subconscious Mind to choose when a setup "feels good" rather than by the correct signals; your Belief System has been tuned over the years to look for investments and take actions that "make sense." A trade that makes rational sense and "feels good" to initiate is usually one where you're trading "with the Herd", or along with the vast masses of Retail traders that all see and act exactly the same, based on the same commonly-available information. Yes, the same ones that the professionals are **taking the other side of the trade on**. Ultimately, this will be a very frustrating experience, because you're doing EVERYTHING in your power to REDUCE risk, however you're actually ADDING risk by allowing your Subconscious Mind to use the same old Belief System that you've used throughout your career, and it absolutely WILL NOT work with respect to trading the market.

There's one statement that I make over and over to my newsletter readers; the very best trades that I take…. the ones that usually work out the best….*are those that feel the worst to take*. At first, you almost want to grab an air-sickness bag and empty your stomach into it when you place the trade, that's what it feels like at the beginning. Taking the other side of the masses of Retail traders FEELS uncomfortable at first, so this is why we need to create a new belief system in your Subconscious Mind. We need to "train it" to welcome the risk, because that's where the rewards are.

One of the great frustrations of beginning investors everywhere....and ESPECIALLY to those who come from successful professional careers....is that the harder that they try to "force" the outcome of a trade, the less successful that they are. We reward hard-drivers in the business world that envision an outcome and then pound everything and everyone around them into submission until that goal is achieved....think of a Head Coach in Football....or a very successful, driven Sales Manager. These same attributes directed towards the Market will be absolutely fruitless, however. Screaming at the charts will do no good, and these successful individuals can make some of the worst traders as they try to apply the same techniques to the Market. You must learn to think differently as the market is not a "linear" world. We need to train that Subconscious Mind on how to think differently about risk and response.

So then, what am I suggesting? Go out and find trades that make absolutely no sense to initiate? No, not quite. Building a new Belief System is like building a wall; we'll create it one brick at a time. And as you'll see, this wall is built one trade at a time.

## How to Train the Brain for Different Beliefs

To be a more profitable investor, we need to "upload" a new Belief System into your Subconscious Mind, one that correctly instructs your RAS to find the right information to produce successful trades. It would be great if it were as simple as just uploading a program into the back of your head, like Neo learned to do in the movie "The Matrix." But we haven't figured out how to do that yet, so we have to do it the hard way. Once you figure this skill out, however....I think you'll really begin to enjoy it, as the benefits extend far beyond the realm of Investing. If you've ever had trouble losing those last ten pounds or quitting a bad habit, you'll soon see that the cure begins by installing a new Belief System.

Now, I wish it were as simple as what many of the "self-help" gurus would have you believe...."*If you think positive, then you'll be positive.*" Sure, it might work to some degree and you'll be a whole lot more pleasant to be around, but unless you start to see RESULTS then your natural skepticism will send you right back to square one. Your old Belief System can be tough to overwrite unless you train it the correct way and start to see benefits.

Basically, what we need to do to "train the brain" is to modify your original Belief System by installing a new one, one that will allow you to profit consistently from the Market. And we'll do that by selectively sending the right information and inputs to it.

Here's the really cool part about this science; your Subconscious mind has no idea if the inputs that it receives are real or not....or true/false. Ever been woken from a dream and it takes you a few moments to realize that you were just dreaming and it was not "real"? Tell that to your Subconscious mind! It didn't know the difference. To it, dreams are no different from the information that it receives when you're awake. You woke with your heart racing, perhaps in a sweat....those are functions that the Subconscious mind governs. Fooled you......

What this means is that the Subconscious Mind can be reprogrammed.

Yep. Since the Subconscious mind cannot judge if something is real or not....nor whether it is true or false.....your job is simply to feed it with the correct inputs to "reprogram" it over time. I'm sure that YOU have made some kind of life change over the years that you didn't originally think that you could accomplish. And it all happened because you were able to "retrain" your Subconscious mind that it needed to occur, and to pave the way for the change. This created a new Belief System and it changed the instructions to the RAS to find the information that supported the change. Success in this endeavor will feed on itself and produce rapid and lasting results.

## So....How Do You Begin to Reprogram Your Mind?

This is the million-dollar question for everyone. The first thing is that you have to WANT to change, and it's best if you're under the pull of inspiration or the push of desperation. You can choose to either continue in the same manner as you already are...in which case you should expect the same old results....or you can decide what you really want and drive towards that direction.

The formula for effective Subconscious change is so simple that it's right under our nose every day:

- Determine what you really want. I mean RE-ALLY, REALLY want.

- Visualize that desire. Make it come alive!

- Schedule time during the day to close your eyes and play this movie in your mind, over and over again.

- Start visualizing your trading success and how you will operate every day.

- Repeat until the vision morphs into reality.

Now this is not exactly easy for the beginner, because what you'll find is that your Conscious mind, with its never-ending logic and objectivity, will start throwing up objections and fill your mind with "clutter." Lots of garbage thoughts like "who are you kidding? You can't make a million dollars!" and "you lost money before, you'll do it again!" That's just the "gatekeeper" doing its job by trying to keep you

where you are already, because the "new" information does not yet synchronize with the existing Belief
System of the Subconscious Mind. This is something
that you'll work through after the first few weeks
with constant reprogramming of your Subconscious
mind. And success begets success; once you see the
results of this in action, then you will want to keep
going and the "gatekeeper" will suddenly become
much more receptive to your positive suggestions.

What is elusive at this critical beginning point is
achieving some success and keeping the process
moving forward. In much the same way that people
get discouraged and stop dieting if they don't lose
ten pounds the first week, you'll need to really apply yourself to learn how to "retrain your brain." As
we pointed out before, most traders will continue
beating their head against the wall for years without
understanding that there are actually much deeper
forces at work inside of their Subconscious Mind that
directly impacts their financial success.

One of the reasons why it can seem so difficult to
achieve this "reprogramming" is because the Subconscious Mind tends to seek pleasure and avoid
pain. For this reason, you'll find many traders making decisions by going "along with the herd" which
is another way of saying that they are making trading decisions based on readily-available information
that everyone else is using. We "seek pleasure" by
entering trades that feel "good" to enter, and everyone else agrees with our actions. (Think "buying at

the highs") We "avoid pain" by either holding onto a losing trade too long, convinced that this "paper loss" will reverse…..or we avoid pain by doing the exact opposite action and take ourselves out of good trades that happen to drop just a little, well above our original "stop."

What you'll need to learn is how to train the Subconscious Mind into thinking that "pleasure" and "pain" will now be based on whether you follow your trading rules or not! (more on this later)

## What Can I do TODAY to Help my Trading?

For all the credit that we give the Subconscious mind, it's very gullible. Think about it; most of you crammed it with all of the wrong ideas and thoughts years ago and your Subconscious mind accepted those thoughts and has been ruling your actions ever since with your current belief system. It can be reprogrammed, however! You can replace the "bad stuff" with strong, empowering thoughts…..via a new Belief System…..starting TODAY.

Here are a couple of exercises to do today:

- **Write a "Day in the Life" paper.** Date it exactly one year from today, and describe your day in full detail, exactly how it unfolds. Make it compelling, vivid, and exciting. Do not limit yourself based on today's perception of what you think is possible. (That's your CURRENT belief system, not the new one you want!) The story should spill out of you as you let your dreams free. Keep working on this paper until it INSPIRES you. Keep reading it and feeling it and very soon you will convince yourself that it's not only possible, but a certainty. You're starting to re-wire your Subconscious mind when you do this exercise.

- **Visualize Your Day.** Sit down in a quiet place before your trading day starts. Close your eyes. Take several deep breaths, focusing on nothing else but your breathing. Think of nothing else, and brush stray thoughts aside. Continue this for a few minutes until a sense of calm comes to you. (Don't fall asleep!) Now start to think about your trading day. Imagine yourself patiently waiting for your setup to come. You are in no hurry, there are no pressures in your life. Your signal comes and you take the setup without hesitation, and it rewards you with a quick profit. Capture this image and practice focusing on this feeling first thing in the morning, and as you go to sleep at night. When you are in the process of trading, emulate the calm and peace that you feel when in this vision. Try to keep your breathing calm and steady, just like in your vision. Once again, you are training your Subconscious mind on how to plan a trade, and how to react during it.

These exercises will help immediately if they are done purposely and regularly. You should feel a new sense of peace and purpose while you trade, and not fear/anxiety in response to risk.

This is such a huge component of effective trading, that you cannot just work on this for a couple of weeks and call yourself "cured." It took you a whole life-time to train your Subconscious brain to its current belief system, so it will take constant maintenance to ensure that you're training that muscle correctly, and forming a new belief system that will instruct the RAS to look for the correct, empowering infor-mation. We will strengthen the correct habits of your new Belief System with the material in subsequent chapters so that this change becomes more durable, lasting, and pervasive. And the first, perhaps most critical thing that we need to accomplish this....is the "rocket fuel" to our efforts that comes when we have PASSION behind our purpose. That is the subject of the next chapter.

## Further Study

I cannot overstate the importance of immersing yourself into this topic as soon as possible, yet I'm not an expert on the human brain; I'm just passing along some of the powerful ideas that I've encountered in my journey. The following materials are resources that I've found helpful to understand this science, and they continue to provide me insight and wonderment:

- *"Secrets of the Millionaire Mind"* by T. Harv Eker - This is a good book but even better CD as he's an entertaining and motivating presenter. This program will help you understand your "Financial Blueprint" which is another way of saying "the financial level of success that you're currently programmed to receive."

- *"The Answer"* by John Assaraf - very interesting book on brain science and extremely applicable to trading. The second half of the book was of less interest since it dealt with running a company.

- *"Having it All"* by John Assaraf - online program to help with retraining your subconscious mind. A how-to manual for Subconscious mind improvement. Good audios for listening on walks.

- *"The Secret"* - a fun and inspiring but somewhat superficial movie that is intended to generate interest in the topic. Find the 20-minute free clip on YouTube first before you order the DVD.

- *"Psycho-Cybernetics"* by Maxwell Maltz - this fifty year-old paperback provides a fas-

cinating view into the world of the Subconscious and how we "see what we want to see"
instead of what's really out there. It's two
bucks for a used copy on amazon.com.

- *"Think and Grow Rich"* **by Napoleon Hill** -
and this one's even older (70+ years) and still
the best. You can either fork out six bucks for
a used paperback, or if you look around you
can find this for free in Apple's iBooks as a
download. This book introduces concepts
that modern-day experts are still trying to
discuss. It's a phenomenal book and I re-read
it at least once a year.

- *"Trading in the Zone"* **by Mark Douglas** -
the author takes a very pragmatic angle at the
underlying causes of poor performance and
blown-out trading accounts. This is a classic
self-help text in trading circles and I re-read it
at least once a year.

# Chapter Six:
# Finding Your Passion

D o you know what it's like to feel unrestrained PASSION for something? Look, I'm not talking about the lovey-dovey "buying flowers for your sweetie" type of passion, although that is certainly one application of it.

No…I'm talking about the "I am so excited that I have to find a bathroom RIGHT NOW otherwise I'm going to burst" kind of passion! The kind of passion where you can't get to sleep at night because your brain is on overdrive thinking about the possibilities…..ever felt that? My guess is that you have at one time or another, and great things come from that energy.

## My Own Story on Passion

When I was in my early thirties I was on top of the world; I had a great job with a terrific, forward-thinking company that was on the razor's edge of innovation and the bleeding edge of the technology at the time. I did very well with that company; I was well-paid, respected for what I did, and advanced quickly up the corporate ladder. And then something changed; the technology that we cornered the market on became a commodity. The world suddenly became more price-sensitive and with it came cost controls, mergers, and infighting. I felt that it was time to leave after ten years, so I sought the next rung up the food chain of employment. I would never again regain that feeling of accomplishment.

Cut to ten years later; I was 42 and was just sort of plodding through life. I woke up one day and found myself working for a manager ten years my junior, a guy who was able to loudly proclaim that he knew all the answers but would secretly come to me for my advice, since I had walked in his shoes not that long ago. I don't know exactly what had happened to derail my career and turn me into a clock-watcher, but it happened with such speed that I felt lost. And then an opportunity came up to attend one of these large arena "motivational" conferences. I figured that a bad day at a conference would beat a good day at the office any day, so I attended and absent-mindedly listened to the first half of the show. Zig Ziglar was a little off his game, and one real-estate expert after another tried to convince me that flipping houses was the easiest thing in the world to make a buck. Yawn. Again, a bad day at a seminar was better than…..

And then it happened. A guy got up and started talking about the stock market and Options and Covered Calls and showing me the signals that he used. Hey WAIT A MINUTE!!! This is COOL!!!! I CAN DO THIS!!! In those thirty minutes I suddenly discovered what it felt to be alive again....my leg bounced as I listened to him, nervous excitement.....when the time came to sign up for his workshop I literally RAN to the table and signed up for the very next live work-shop, two days later. They gave me the home-study materials right there and I immediately drove home and read them ALL that night and the next day until I attended the workshop.

That began an 18-month journey of discovery for me which culminated the day that I handed in my no-tice and quit my good-paying, safe, boring job for the life of a full-time trader. That day at that seminar, I had discovered my PASSION for working with fi-nancial markets, that continues to this day. Without that drive, that fire in my belly....I would not have accomplished my goal of doing this.

## Running Through a Brick Wall

Another moment which was etched in my memory came much earlier in my life, when I was about twen-ty. I was a tech-savvy but unfocused young man trying to figure out what I would do in life. One of my passions at the time was music, specifically the technical side of it. Working in a recording studio ap-peared to be a dream job, so I signed up for a series of workshops on how to do live recording engineering and production. What a gorgeous studio...there were two main studios, each with a control room flanked on either side by a "live" room with hardwood floors designed to enhance the natural echo, and a "dead" room that was lined with carpet and foam walls and reduced the interference between instruments. In the control room was a sound board with 48 channels feeding 2" Scotch 3M Recording tape running at 30 inches per second. For a kid that was used to recording music on a cassette tape, this was Nirvana.

Going to the studio every week for a session was absolute heaven, a dream. And one day I bumped into Arnie, the CEO/Founder of that studio, and we had a little chat. I finally couldn't contain myself, and gushed, "This is the coolest place I've been to in my life. How did you DO this? How were you able to build this studio?" His response is something I've carried with me my entire life: "Once you know what you want, it's like anything else. You have to be willing to run through a brick wall to get what you want."

Without belief, a Karate student cannot break a board without hurting themselves. Without passion, you cannot run through that brick wall to attain what you really want. If it were that easy, then everyone would be doing it. Trust me, they're not. Find your own brick wall and break through it.

## Finding The Rage to Master

Once you have passion for your purpose, it's not going to lead to success if you just bounce off the walls and flame out by spreading your efforts everywhere. You need to adopt a "rage to master" by channeling your energy into excelling at a small list of activities or strategies. This quote is attributable to Brett Steenbarger's excellent book, "Enhancing Trader Performance" and is one of my favorites. When I first started trading, I became knowledgeable in many different Options strategies, however the only person that was making money was my broker. I was a "Jack of All Trades and a Master of None." It was not until I focused my attention on one strategy and adopting a "rage to master" that one strategy.....that success finally came.

That "Rage to Master" started innocently enough; I followed a trade by a popular newsletter service that laid out a very logical, well-constructed bearish trade on a home builder. My bearish position was located well above all-time price highs for that stock, and I was confident in their analysis. So confident, in fact, that I used a very large position in my retirement account.

And then the price began to rise, attacking my position and getting closer and closer to breaking into all-time new highs for that stock! I could not sleep, I twisted myself into knots wondering what to do. After several back-and-forth exchanges with the newsletter, their final piece of advice was "well, you should have gotten out yesterday."

I was furious; I felt betrayed. For a trade to start out with such promise, one that made such LOGICAL sense to begin with….to eventually fail spectacularly was beyond my comprehension. I could have channeled this rage to quit in a huff and never to return; many take this route. I chose the alternate route; I directed this anger and rage inward and challenged myself to come up with a better "defense" for a position like this. I spent weeks at it and studied everything that I could…I found out that I was actually pioneering some of the research and effort in this field. Before too long, I had taken this bad experience and turned it into a distinct advantage, as I had MASTERED this form of defense. I had found the Rage to Master this trade and it directly led to me leaving the employment world and working for myself in the markets.

"If you come to a fork in the road, take it. "

- Yogi Berra

## Go Speed-Dating for Strategies

If you spend any time checking your email, you'll no doubt receive many different compelling promotional campaigns on different techniques and strategies, all claiming to be the best. And maybe they ARE the best…for that trader. What you have to find…is the one for YOU. I am a firm believer that there is no one "BEST" strategy, there is no "Holy Grail" strategy out there that works every time.....however, there is one "best" strategy for YOU. I have seen traders absolutely slog through a grueling effort to learn a specific style of trading, just because someone else told them to. They will never make any progress at that strategy, simply because they will never attain the "Rage to Master" and have the velocity to ram through that brick wall. Slow and steady will not win the race if you don't have the PASSION for what you're doing.

I have had many instances of this; for a brief period of time I took a huge risk, moved to Chicago away from my family, slept in someone's closet and became a "Prop Trader." A Proprietary Trader is one who trades a firm's money using a specific "proprietary" algorithm. It's no exaggeration to say that I've never been more bored. I kept a laptop with a charting program up, which was an anomaly in that office as no one used charts....and my gaze was constantly drawn back to that laptop and those gorgeous patterns coming up time after time on those charts. It wasn't long before I decided that I would never attain the passion for that specific type of prop trading, and that I was better off pursuing something else.

This is what you must do, similar to those that "speed date" in today's world. Try something for a short period of time. Learn about it, don't make any huge investments in education or platforms, but TRY IT. See if it fits your personality; does it give you an uncontrolled RAGE TO MASTER this strategy? It had better, otherwise you're better off continuing your hunt to find something that works for you.

Don't forget - it only takes ONE strategy, and ONE instrument to build a winning edge and achieve mastery. Being a Jack of All Trades will likely lead to poor performance by being a Master of None. Speaking of Mastery, we now move to the next chapter where we'll discuss the roadmap that everyone takes to attain that level.

# Chapter Seven:
# The Trader's Progression

**Where are you in your trading career?**

E veryone comes to the world of investing & trading from a different background. Some of you have just signed up with an online broker and have experimented with different forms of trading instruments. Others will have several years of successful Stock or Futures trading experience but are looking to diversify into different forms of trading. Honestly, where are you today?

And yes, believe me, it's a CAREER. Those who treat trading as a hobby will pay for it like a hobby. Those who truly treat this profession as a career will open themselves to being paid like a professional, if they follow the right steps. And for those in the trading education business, we're all guilty to some degree of trying to downplay the role that "experience" has when making decisions. Things that come easily to me today are a direct result of them being "hard" at one time in my career, and learning to get past that point. As a specific example, this morning the Dow Jones Industrial Average dropped almost 1100 points from the prior day's closing price...that was a 6.6% move and most of it occurred in the premarket/ overnight and the first hour of the day. It goes without saying that a neophyte investor would view that drop with a deer-in-the-headlights expression, and would probably panic and sell into the low of the day to "cut his losses." The net result of my effort was to make money today, but I had to earn the right to profit from a day like this by "paying my dues" over the years. When I began, I was the one contributing to others' accounts.

So part of this journey we can write down to experience and practice; the more you get of both, the faster that you will progress. But there's something more than that; if it was just time alone that differentiated the investor, then you'd see a lot more 70-year old millionaires. It's not only the time that you put in, but what you DO with that time. Like everything else, your path to consistent profitability will follow a **progression**...from outright Novice to Expert. There are many models to quantify this progression, but the best one that I've come across was written by Bo Yoder (www.boyoder.com); his model is comprised of six distinct stages in a trader's development:

## Stage One – Mystification

This is where the neophyte trader begins. He has little or no understanding of market structure. He has no concept of the interrelationship among markets, much less between markets and the economy. Price charts are a meaningless mish-mash of colored lines and squiggles that look more like a painting from the MOMA than anything that contains information. Anyone who can make even a guess about price direction based on this tangle must be using black magic, or voodoo.

## Stage Two – The Hot Pot Stage

You scan the markets every day. After a while (sometimes a good long while), you notice a particular phenomenon which pops up regularly and seems to "work" pretty well. You focus on this pattern. You begin to find more and more instances of it and all of them work! Your confidence in the pattern grows and you decide to take it the very next time it appears. You take it, and almost immediately your stop is hit, and you're underwater for the total amount of your stop-loss.

So you back off and study this pattern further. And the very next time it appears, it works. Again and again. So you decide to try again. And you take the full hit on your stop loss.

Practically everyone goes through this, but few understand that this is all part of the win-lose cycle. They do not yet understand that loss is an inevitable part of any system/strategy/method/whathaveyou, that is, there is no such thing as a 100% win approach. When they gauge the success of a particular pattern or setup, they get caught up in the win cycle. They don't wait for the "lose" cycle to see how long it lasts or what the win/lose pattern is. Instead, they keep touching the pot and getting burned, never understanding that it's not the pot (pattern/setup) that's the problem, but a failure on their part to understand that it's the heat from the stove (the market) that they're paying no attention to whatsoever. So instead of trying to understand the nature of thermal transfer (the market), they avoid the pot (the pattern), moving on to another pattern/setup without bothering to find out whether or not the stove is on.

## Stage Three – The Cynical Skepticism Stage

You've studied so hard and put so much effort into your trading and this "universal failure in the patterns only when you take them" causes you to feel betrayed by the market, the books, the materials, and the gurus you tried to learn from. Everybody claims their ideas lead to profitability, but every time you take a trade, it's a loser, even though the setups all worked perfectly before you played them.

And since one of the most painful experiences is to fail when success looks easy, this embarrassment is transformed into anger: anger at the gurus, anger at the vendors, anger at the writers, the seminars, the courses, the brokers, the market makers, the specialists, the "manipulators." What's the point in trying to analyze and improve your own trading when there are so many dark forces out to get you?

This excuse-driven blame game is a dead-end viewpoint, and explains a lot of what you find on message boards. Those who can't pull themselves out of it will quit.

## Stage Four – The Squiggle Trader Stage

If you don't quit, you'll move into the "squiggle trader" phase. Since you failed with patterns and so on, you figure there's some "secret weapon", a "holy grail" that's known to the select few, something that will help you filter out all those bad trades. Once you find this magical key, your profits will explode and you'll achieve every dream you ever had.

You begin an obsessive study of every method and every indicator that is new to you. You buy every book, attend every course, sign up for every newsletter and advisory service, register for every trading website and every chat room. You buy more elaborate software. You buy off-the-shelf systems. You spend whatever it takes to buy success.

Unfortunately, you stack so much onto your charts that you become paralyzed. With so many inputs, you can't make a decision, particularly since they rarely agree. So you focus on those which agree with the direction of the trade you've taken (or, if you're the fearful sort, you look only for those which will prove to you how much of a loser you think you are).

This is all characteristic of scared money. Without a genuine acceptance of the fact of loss and of the risks involved in trading, you flit around like a butterfly in search of anything or anybody who will tell you that you know what you're doing. This serves two purposes: (1) it transfers to others the responsibility for the trade and (2) it shakes you out of trades as your indicators begin to conflict. The MACD says buy, the STO says sell. The ADX says the market is trending, the OBV says it's overbought. By the end of the day, your brain is jelly.

This process can be useful if the trader learns from it what is popular, i.e., what other traders are doing, and, if he lasts, how to trade traps and panic/ euphoria. And even though he may decide that much of it is crap, he will, if he doesn't slip back into the Cynical Skepticism Stage, have a more profound appreciation -- achieved through personal experience -- of what is sensible and logical and what is nonsense. He might also learn something more about the kind of trader he is, what "style" suits him best, learn to distinguish between what is desirable and what is practical.

But the vast majority of traders never leave this stage. They spend their "careers" searching for the answer, and even though they may eventually achieve piddling profits (if they don't, they will of course eventually no longer be trading), they never become truly successful, and this has its own insidious consequences.

## Stage Five – The Inwardly-Bound Stage

The trader who is able to pry himself out of Stage Four uses his experiences there productively. The trader learns, as stated earlier, what styles, techniques, tactics are popular. But instead of focusing entirely on what's "out there", he begins to ask himself some questions:

What exactly does he want? What is he trying to accomplish?

What sort of trading makes the most sense to him? Long or intermediate term trading? Short-term trading? Day-trading? Trend-trading? Scalping? Which is most comfortable?

What instrument -- futures, stocks, ETFs, bonds, options -- provides the range and volatility he requires but is not outside his risk tolerance? Did he learn anything at all about indicators in Stage Four that he might be able to use?

And so he "auditions" all of this in order to determine what suits him, taking all that he has learned so far and experimenting with it..

He begins to incorporate the "scientific method" into his efforts in order management. He learns the value of curiosity, of detached interest, of persistence and perseverance, of taking bits and pieces from here and there in order to fashion a trading plan and strategy that are uniquely his, one in which he has complete confidence because he has tested it thoroughly and knows from his own experience that it is consistently profitable.

He accepts fully the responsibility for his trades, including the losses, which is to say that he understands that losses are inevitable and unavoidable. Rather than be thrown by them, he accepts them for what they are, a part of the natural course of business. He examines them, of course, in order to determine whether or not some error was made, particularly one that can be corrected, though true trading errors are rare. But, if not, he simply shrugs off the loss and goes on about his business. He understands, after all, that he is in control of his risk in the market.

He doesn't rant about his broker or the specialist or the market maker or that vast conspiracy of everyone who's trying to cheat him out of his money. He doesn't attempt revenge against the market. He doesn't fret. He doesn't fume. He doesn't succumb to hope, fear, greed. Impulsive, emotional trades are gone. Instead, he just trades.

## Stage Six – Mastery

At this level, the trader achieves an almost Zen-like trading state. Planning, analysis, research are the focus of his time and his effort. When the trading day opens, he's ready for it. He's calm, he's relaxed, he's centered.

Trading becomes effortless. He is thoroughly familiar with his plan. He knows exactly what he will do in any given situation, even if the doing means exiting immediately upon a completely unexpected development. He understands the inevitability of loss and accepts it as a natural part of the business of trading. No one can hurt him because he's protected by his rules and his discipline.

He is sensitive to and in tune with the ebb and flow of market behavior and the natural actions and reactions to it that his research has taught him will optimize his edge. He is "available." He doesn't have to know what the market will do next because he knows how he will react to anything the market does and is confident in his ability to react correctly.

He understands and practices "active inaction", knowing exactly what it is he wants, exactly what it is he's looking for, and waiting, patiently, for exactly the right opportunity. If and when that opportunity presents itself, he acts decisively and without hesitation, then waits, patiently, again, for the next opportunity.

He does not convince himself that he is right. He watches price movement and draws his conclusions. When market behavior changes, so do his tactics. He acknowledges that market movement is the ultimate truth. He doesn't try to outsmart or outguess it.

He is, in a sense, outside himself, acting as his own coach, asking himself questions and explaining to himself without rationalization what he's waiting for, what he's doing, reminding himself of this or that, keeping himself centered and focused, taking distractions in stride. He doesn't get overexcited about winning trades; he doesn't get depressed about losing trades. He accepts that price does what it does and the market is what it is.

His performance has nothing to do with his self-worth. It is during this stage that the "intuitive" sense begins to manifest itself. As infrequent as it may be, he learns to experiment with it and to build trust in it.

And at the end of the day, he reviews his work, makes whatever adjustments are necessary, if any, and begins his preparation for the following day, satisfied with himself for having traded well.

The knowledge proved through research that a particular price pattern or market behavior offers an acceptable level of predictability and risk to reward to provide a consistently profitable outcome over time.

## Where Were You?

What stage were you in? By the time that most traders understand that Mindset and Discipline hold the key to trading success, they are soundly stuck in stage four. In fact, most traders that I meet with some formal trading education and a fair amount of trading experience will be in **stage four**. That's fine, you're just in the middle of the bell curve.

It's also my experience that you cannot "skip" a stage; everyone will pass through these stages sequentially. The driven and focused student spends less time on the earlier stages, and more time in stage five as they patiently attain the skills necessary for Mastery, stage six.

And the more that you dedicate yourself to this profession, the deeper that you will allow yourself to enter into the study of the Trading Mindset. You will actually begin to enjoy the journey instead of fighting it.

So honestly, it really doesn't matter what stage you begin in. You're going to be doing this for a number of years, right? Does a prospective Brain Surgeon quit medical school in the first month because they haven't yet attained the skills necessary to check someone's pulse correctly? If they do quit, it's because that person didn't have the right perspective and a long-term vision of what it would take.

So you might not yet be a successful trader, because you're in an early stage of your development......that's absolutely fine. What counts is your determination, and your vision of what you want to achieve; remember what we just said about having the passion to break through a brick wall.

## A Simplified Version of the Trader's Progression

One of the unbreakable tenets in trading is that the more honest you are with yourself, the faster that you can break the bonds of non-performance by truly tackling and correcting what is broken. Far too many students that I talk to claim to be in stage 5 or 6 of Bo's Progression, yet I see the same characteristics in their performance and self-denial that are contained in the earlier stages. With that in mind, perhaps these folks are projecting forward what they *want* instead of understanding what *is*. That's OK, because as we already showed in the preceding chapters, it's important to at least start with a vision of what you want. (But the faster that you're able to separate fiction from reality, the faster that you'll progress!)

What might work better for investors that are misidentifying their stage in the Progression is to use a simplified version of this identification tree:

- **Stage One:** In this stage as an investor, you end up losing lots of money and blow out one (or several) accounts.

- **Stage Two:** When you progress to this stage, you stop losing large amounts of money and stop blowing up accounts, however at best you are a "scratch" or break-even trader.
- **Stage Three:** Once you enter this stage, you start effortlessly earning large amounts of income.

Once again, you cannot skip steps in this progression. I hesitate to feature this simplified version of the Trader's Progression because any trader that's been underway for a few months will magically score a big winning trade, then automatically assume that they've graduated to Stage Three or Four of Yoder's Progression.

It's a very natural progression that traders first focus on how much they can WIN which is the discovery phase of Stage One, which leads them eventually to Stage Two because they realize that the whole concept of Risk Management is an acquired skill and usually comes down the road after some large losses. And Stage Three does not present itself until you have effectively trained your Subconscious Mind to accept success, as we discussed in the previous chapters.

## Where Do You Want to Go?

And this is where the part about Vision comes in.

This question really is aimed at two levels:

What level of trading expertise do you want to attain? What will trading success mean to you?

For the first question, by now you should be honestly identifying what level that you have attained, and are wondering what it will take to get to the next level and beyond. Good. But beyond that is the second question....where do you want this trading success to take you? And what will you do to get there?

The answer to these questions are already imprinted in your Belief System and your Subconscious Mind. It's already thinking thoughts like:

- "I feel guilty about taking money from others"

- "I'll bet that this is hard and I probably won't get it"

If you find yourself "stuck" at any one level and cannot get to the next, chances are very strong that your Belief System needs work. But there's also the strong possibility that you just don't have the FRAMEWORK to create success; all the will in the world will not make you a good driver if you don't grab the steering wheel. And that's what the next chapter is about, learning how to manage YOURSELF.

# Chapter Eight:
# Managing the Trader

So far, we've started to train our Subconscious Mind for success, we've found what we're passionate about and focused our efforts in that direction, and we just determined what level of the Trader's Progression that we fit into. We're starting to develop some structure for our development for our role as a Trader. There is one thing about "becoming" a trader that no one talks about, yet is critical: How do you manage YOURSELF?

Think about it….odds are, you've gone from grade school education to some type of college, eventually landing a job and working for someone else. The center of the bell curve of students that I work with have been employees of one form or another for their entire professional lives, with all of the benefits and frustrations that come with that distinction. *But at no time have they ever had to run their own business!* For many of these folks, the last time that they ran something on their own was a lemonade stand in their front yard or delivering the morning newspaper.

So now you've achieved your dream by becoming an independent trader/investor, even if you're doing it on the side, and there are NO RULES and NO MANAG-ERS telling you what you can and can't do. This is the blessing - and the curse - of running your own enter-prise. Ultimate freedom, yet no guidance. Is there any wonder why so many traders fail at this? It's taken me a lifetime of lessons to get to the point where I can run my own trading business, so let me cover the high points in this chapter.

## The Vision

Let's start by first discussing your goals and your Vision for being a "trader," or self-directed investor. The classic image that we've all been programmed to think about is someone laying on a beach, laptop in one hand and a drink in the other, casually checking on their portfolio while the dollars roll in.

That's kind of the dream, right? For most of us, that would be a vision of success. And perhaps it is for you as well, but let me caution you that *you need to earn that ability* to trade from your hammock. I have been around many traders of the "Mastery" level and not one did I meet while they were guzzling a Mai-Tai. They all worked very hard at their jobs and were absolutely in love with what they did. In fact, I would say without exception that they *worked much harder* than the novice traders. It's pretty easy to draw a conclusion from this.

Sure, there's absolutely a time for play. And many times it does help to get away from the daily beat of the Market, and get a fresh perspective on it when you return. But let's get this straight up front: **trading is serious business**. You're stepping into the lion cage with the best in the world! The quote that I've heard over the years still rings true: "Treat this like a business and it'll pay you like a business. Treat it like a hobby and it'll cost you money like a hobby."

## Having Access to the Market

Many students that I work with bemoan the fact that they have jobs and do not have full-time access to the market; as we'll see, that's not necessarily an impediment to success, depending on the style of trading that you do. Yes, it only takes me about five to ten minutes a day to place most of my trades and in general, I'm not glued to the screen. If I need to run an errand, I have that freedom. I can do errands as needed in the middle of the day. But I am present and engaged and I always know what the Market is doing, and am ready to act should it be necessary. And I have earned that right to be in control of my day by first doing my "homework" which allows me to be proactive.

Circumstances differ for all Traders; some pursue trading in a Full-time manner surrounded by screens and to-the-tick data, while most do it "on the side" while pursuing outside employment. How can a part-time trader compete with a full-time trader?

The answer is probably different than you'd think. In Nicholas Darvas' book "How I Made $2,000,000 in the Stock Market," he detailed how he traveled the world as a performer, all the while swing trading NYSE stocks with stock quotes delayed by several days. Bear in mind that this was about 60 years ago! Darvas' secret was that he developed his own system, continually tuned it, and actually found that the further away he was from the noise and rumors of Wall Street, the better his performance was.

The Darvas story has inspired millions over the years because it reminds them that if someone can be thousands of miles away, completely disconnected from the Markets, with delayed feeds....then someone who is perhaps hours away from a quote still stands a pretty good chance to succeed as well.

It's all a question of how you manage your time.

Now keep in mind that you're going up against some of the brightest and most highly paid minds in the field...talent on the Street doesn't come cheap, so you're going to have to outwork your opponent if you want "Your Fair Share" of profits....and do it with less time and market access than they have.

Because of these constraints, how you utilize your time will be, of course, absolutely crucial.

## Turn Off the TV

Even before I began my career as a full-time trader, I would take the occasional holiday from work to trade from home. Ah, it was bliss! This was right in line with my vision of how life would be as I pursued my goal. And the first thing that I would do is to wheel that TV into my room and fire up CNBC or whatever "Stock TV" channel that I could receive.

It was exciting...between the pre-market analysis with heavy hitters, to the on-floor reporters who made you feel like you were "right there"....I felt like I was really tied into the pulse of the Market.

Yet it didn't help a bit. Performance on those "trade at home" days was abysmal. (The Percy Hedger story at the beginning of this book may or may not have roots in my own reality!)

Only after I spent a few years doing this did I really understand the subtle dynamics at work. "Experts" were "talking their book" up, with a hidden agenda to bid up the price so that they could sell into it. "Breaking News" was, in actuality, already anticipated for the most part and professionals would use the event to sell into it. You might have heard the expression, "buy the rumor, sell the news." And then there was just the overall "Cheerleader" effect, where there was an underlying bias to whip up "the Herd" and get everyone moving in the same direction.

In general, the masses that follow the Stock Market will always pick the wrong direction. And watching CNBC, or any other "stock media" channel, was making me part of the "Herd" that was getting continually "faded" by the professionals. And for the reasons that we went into earlier in this book, the Subconscious Mind always likes to trade along with the Herd, in order to seek pleasure and avoid pain.

So be like the professionals; you will need objective data sources to maintain your edge, like any trader will. But be quick to be skeptical about someone else's opinion; falling in line with the Herd will be at your own peril.

## Do your Homework

The Number One, Unpardonable, Cardinal Sin for every trader is to get to the end of a trading day and say "Ooops. There it was." You missed a signal. An obvious entry point....a moving average cross.....a trendline break....a green arrow, whatever it was, the Train has Left the Station and you're not on it.

You didn't do your homework. You weren't prepared. You decided to tackle a trading day by "shooting from the hip"; this is a classic rookie mistake and unfortunately even one that experienced traders can fall victim to if they get complacent. How many times have you heard conversations with other traders about a missed move? How OBVIOUS does a past move look now that you have the benefit of history to look at it? (And the number one sales technique of high-priced educational firms!)

The ONLY way that you can make effective decisions on the "hard right edge" where the future is unknown is to be PREPARED. And that doesn't happen without doing your Homework.

This "Homework" will be different depending on what your trading strategy and style is, but here are a few classic examples:

- Stock traders should be building a weekly watchlist preferably over the weekend.

- All traders should know relative areas of Support and Resistance for the charts and the primary timeframes that they trade.

- Stock and Options traders must know Earnings and Dividend dates if they play individual stocks.

- Option traders must know what actions that they might need to do to "defend" their positions tomorrow should the price go up, down, or sideways.

- All traders should know dates and times for economic announcements or any other event that generates volatility and risk.

- Any trader holding a live position must know specifically what their exit point is, or the trigger point for any other defensive measures.

- Any trader must pre-identify any possible entry on the charts and timeframes that they follow.

- Intraday traders should know shorter-term levels of support and resistance, daily pivot readings, or any other important area where action might be required.

There are many tools that one can use to build some structure into their daily homework, such as spreadsheets, pre-printed templates, white boards with organized fields, or anything else that you can build and maintain. The objective here is CONSISTENCY; you should be going through the same process, day after day, making sure that you don't miss anything and you are 100% prepared for how you're going to approach the next trading day.

WHEN you actually do this should be up to you and your schedule; some are night owls, others are early birds. The point here is that you should never be trading unless you have done your Homework and have "earned the right" to risk your capital.

## Plan your Day

Ever felt like you got to the end of the day, and you're not sure what happened? What you accomplished? I'm sure that you've heard the expression, "If you fail to plan, then plan to fail!" It sounds a little severe, but it's true.

Planning your Day goes hand in hand with the Homework that we just discussed; make sure that your trading homework is done well before the opening bell, so that you know EXACTLY what you will do in any market circumstance.

And planning your day really should be a smaller extension of the Trader's Business Plan that we'll discuss in the next chapter. The Business Plan is really pulling together the macro level goals and strategies that you intend to accomplish in a specific timeframe, so your daily planning becomes a micro extension of that business plan.

Look, if you wanted to lose 20 pounds.....unless you're an MMA fighter you probably can not and should not accomplish this in one day. But if you take daily action towards a larger goal, then you can incrementally make progress towards it and arrive at your destination before you expect to.

And everything related to the trading business occurs in the same manner; you will make incremental progress daily in your knowledge and experience, eventually leading to your performance goals.

Look, I'm not going to try to pretend that I'm Stephen Covey, you can find plenty of self-help resources out there that focus on time management and how to squeeze every little effective nugget out of a 24 hour period. All that I'd like to accomplish for you in this section is to get you to use your time effectively during the day so that you can FOCUS on the task at hand, which is pulling consistent income from the Market. There are simply too many variables that make trading a challenge already; *your own personal execution should never be one of them.*

So to get you to plan your day a little better, we need to look to Automate some of your tasks, as well as filter some of the things that you're working on by identifying High and Low Value activities.

## Automate

If you're like most traders, you probably don't confine yourself to watching one chart, trading one strategy, entering trades once a month, etc. Most of us are multi-taskers and are trying to leverage our trading capital across several different strategies; this makes us well-diversified.

What this diversification and complexity means is that there is a relatively large probability that we're going to drop the ball on something! Have you ever traded over an economic announcement that you had forgotten about? Ever forget to close down a position prior to Options Expiration? Missed an entry on a signal because you had popped down the hall to grab a drink? Now that you've spent all that time preparing for the trading day by doing your Homework, don't drop the ball with your execution!

Realistically, life is much "busier" than it was in Darvas' day. We all have many more places to be, many more things to do, and more interruptions during the day than we did even a few short years ago. If you challenge this notion, then just compare today's handwriting vs. that practiced 50 years ago....people used to have the time to dedicate to small details that they no longer do.

But in this whirlwind of electronic interference comes our salvation; you just have to jump in and embrace the tools. Take the time to learn how to help these tools AUTOMATE the details so that you can use your brain for processing, and not storage.

Here are some specific examples that you can consider:

- **Automate Calendar Warnings** – when you do your homework, make sure that you understand the dates and times of upcoming announcements, or any other date of importance. Make sure that you capture that event right there and then by placing a warning into a device that you use every day, such as an Outlook or Google calendar event, or possibly even to program the warning into your charting program.

- **Automate Entry and Exit conditions** – entries and exit signals can occur through any number of technical or price-based conditions; make sure that your broker platform or charting program notifies you! Alarms can be set on trend-line breaks, emails can be generated if specific price levels are hit, etc. These levels should be programmed in during your quiet "Homework" period.

- **Portable Broker interfaces** – it used to be that a laptop PC was the ultimate in portability and automation; now you can take an entire broker interface with your on your Smart-Phone or iPad/tablet. If you can't automate the trade 100% through your tools, then take your tools with you to manage the trade. This is especially useful for those trading while at a job, where opening up a full screen in a work environment would be inappropriate.... yet a quick peek at a SmartPhone is discrete and generally does not constitute a personal/ work conflict.

## The Pareto Principle

You already know about the "Pareto Principle," you just might not know the name behind it.

The principle simply states that "80% of effects come from 20% of the causes." It has also been called the "80/20 rule." When used in "time management" it means that 80% of the results that you generate are coming from 20% of your efforts (your time)....and that 20% of the results are coming from 80% of our time!

So the question is... What are we doing with the 80% of our time that is not generating any results? You guessed it, we are wasting it! This is where planning your day can help to give you a concrete set of activities and prioritize them so you can get more done!

First off, what are we doing with the 80% of our time? Wasting it! Do these sound familiar?:

- Check your e-mail 50 times per day?
- Surf the net out of boredom?
- If you are in an office-how many days do you come in and shuffle some papers on your desk, check you e-mail, stare at the screen, take a break to talk to other co-workers, etc,

just to pass the time by?

- Update your Facebook or check on your "friends?"
- Take "extended" lunches?

I think everyone has been guilty of this at some point; this is where the 80/20 Pareto principle can change your life.

Your mission is find out what 20% of activities that you are doing that are generating 80% of your results and go spend your time in those activities, getting better at them, and finding other activities like them. These are what we call "High Value Activities." What are the High Value Activities when it comes to your trading, and how can you do MORE of them?

You might also take this opportunity to examine your trading as well; you might find that the majority of your profits are coming from a small number of specific strategies. Using the Pareto principle, it might make sense to focus more of your time towards those winning strategies instead of the losing ones. Focus on what you're good at, because you'll attack the task with passion.

## A Trader's Best Friend

....is a job. Yes, believe it or not, having a day job is actu-

ally a blessing in disguise for most. I know, I know....
the whole idea is to get RID of your job and work from
home, or fund your retirement.

I do speak from experience here. During my first few
months of self-employment, I had fortunately wan-
dered into a very quiet and benign Market that wan-
dered sideways for months. It was all too easy to bring
income in every month.

Then...disaster struck!

The market underwent an overdue correction and all
of a sudden I was looking at a losing month. I cannot
overemphasize the amount of stress that you will be
under trying to trade when you know that your ability to feed and shelter your family is being threatened.
Recall that the Subconscious mind calls all the shots
at the end of the day, and its principle goal is to either
seek pleasure or avoid pain.

Whenever you avoid pain, you will automatically
trade "with the Herd" and it's very likely that you
will then undergo even more stress as you start to lose
more trades. This is where many well-meaning traders auger into the ground and blow out their accounts.
They announced to the world not three months ago
that they were going to be a trader, and before you
know it they are crawling back to their previous job
with their tails between their legs, seeking some form
of employment.

Fortunately my situation didn't implode and I was able

to learn valuable lessons from it. And one that I would like to pass along to you...is to stay employed for as long as you can stand it. Make yourself a "departure plan" that gives you more than enough capital to fall back on, to the point where the loss of a trade does not generate an emotional response. The only capital that you will be able to effectively trade and place at risk.... is the capital that you don't care about. Any "heat" on a trade that causes you to feel threatened, will invoke the pleasure/pain response from your Subconscious mind. And we all know how that will end.

Now, many folks reading this might not have that opportunity - perhaps they are recently laid-off, unemployed, disabled, or sidelined in any number of ways. I can't address your specific situation here, however I would make yourself aware of the huge number of opportunities that one can take advantage of for self-employment and/or contracted labor. One example might be setting yourself up as an Uber driver, working at night. Another might be working as remote technical or phone support from home. These days, if you have an internet connection and a computer, you have an almost infinite number of ways to add value and earn a paycheck without necessarily "working" in a traditional office/factory/warehouse environment.

## Summary - Trader Management

Yes, there's a LOT to work on, isn't there? It's not easy to go from an environment where you have little freedom in a typical "job"....to one where you have

ULTIMATE freedom, even if you're just trading on the side. Understanding how to manage yourself and your time, how to control your opinions and bias, thinking like the "smart money", and how to make sure that you've effectively prepared yourself for your trading day is the true mark of a professional. And you must act like a professional before you can call yourself one, so there's no better time than today to get started. Now, if we're going to call your trading a "business," then we need to create a plan so that we can plan for success.

# Chapter Nine:
# Business & Trading Plans

Let's do a quick reset of where we are with our mission…..

- We've established that we need a new Belief System so that our RAS is out seeking information that will make our trading successful.

- We've started to visualize what success looks like and what our "perfect day" resembles. We're starting to reprogram our Belief System.

- We've identified the elements (and perhaps the strategies) that get us passionate about our trading business.

- We've identified what stage of the Trader Progression that we're at.

- And we've started to take steps to run our trading as a "business."

If you're going to run this venture as a BUSINESS and not just an expensive hobby, then you need a

**Trader's Business Plan**. Far too many traders just wade into this business thinking of all of the riches waiting in that pot of gold at the end of the rainbow, only to find that the rainbow dims as they lose their way. Name a Fortune 500 business that doesn't have an annual plan in place...you won't find one! The shareholders demand it for those companies, as your stakeholders should demand of you. And as we said before, "If you fail to plan, then plan to fail," ....there is a lot of truth to that phrase.

What should be included in a Trader's Business Plan? We've found the best example of one to be in John Carter's book, *Mastering the Trade*. His sample plan is built by answering the following questions:

- What do I want to accomplish by trading this year?
- What Markets and instruments am I going to trade?
- What specific strategies am I going to use to trade these Markets?
- How much money am I going to allocate to each trading strategy?
- How will I rank and track my trades?
- What are my drawdown rules?
- What are my profit rules? (Daily/weekly/monthly goals)
- What is my trading environment?
- What are my rewards if I hit my goals?

- Is there a charity that I will support if I hit my goals?
- How will I maintain this to "stay on plan" throughout the year?
- What am I doing about my physical health?
- What Trading Education Goals/Plans do I have?

Building a Trader's Business Plan is not a difficult task, and you don't have to be perfect your first try. That's what the Strategy Development Cycle is for, shown below:

Goals

Rules

Strategy
Development
Cycle

Corrections

Results

You start this cycle by specifying Goals, which then are implemented through Rules. Eventually you'll see results, after which you can determine whether or not your results will lead to you meeting your Goals.....and if not, you make Corrections.

Repeat this cycle and you're now running a Continuous Improvement Process just like any Fortune

500 corporation. After all, they do it, why shouldn't you? Your Trader's Business Plan needs to be constantly evaluated through a Development Cycle like this. Most Traders' Business Plans get written during a bowl game on January 1st and are collecting dust within a month. Use the same cycle….Goals/Rules/Results/Corrections to keep you plan current and run your trading operation like a Global corporation!

## What Do I Do With a Business Plan?

Think of a business plan as a map from point "A" to point "B." If you try to get to point "B" by sticking your nose in the map the entire time, chances are you'll go off course because you'll miss a turn. Yet if you never consult with the map, how will you know if you're on course or not? Running a business like an "independent investing business" is much the same; you need to start by outlining a destination…..where do you want to go? What are your goals? The Business Plan helps with this because it outlines the process on how to GET THERE.

As I mentioned before, this business plan does not have to be perfect nor does it have to be "right" the first time out. Perhaps where you thought you wanted to go is not really where you want to go after all. Or perhaps you were too aggressive with your goals; that's OK, many newer investors are. But the point here is that if the Plan is wrong, EDIT it! Go ahead and modify the plan, it's just like turning the steering wheel in your car. A car was never meant to go only in a straight line, so don't have the same expectations with your business.

At a minimum, dust off your plan once a month to see if you're on track. (Hint: set a calendar reminder and don't skip the process!)

## How Is This Different From a Trading Plan?

An actual TRADING PLAN is quite different from a BUSINESS PLAN. The Trading Plan lists the specifics on how you will execute and manage your individual trades, per strategy. Here are some example points to include in each trading strategy in your Trading plan:

- **Description** - What is the strategy? Does it have a name?
- **Edge** - What "edge" do you have in your strategy that should allow you to profit consistently?
- **Instruments** - What trading instruments will you trade this with? Stocks, futures, options, or Forex pairs?
- **Entry Conditions** - Under what specific criteria will you enter the trade?

- **Entry Timing -** Are there specific timing conditions that affect the entry conditions, such as time of day, number of days to expiration, etc.?

- **Position Sizing -** How much risk will you take per trade? Are there criteria that you can specify to quantify the position size?

- **Defense and Exits -** Will you plan any "defensive" actions to take if the position is under duress? What are your stops? Profit targets?

- **Misc Factors -** Are there any miscellaneous factors to consider, such as earnings dates, dividend payouts, or news-related items?

- **Strategy Maintenance -** How will you adjust this strategy going forward? How will you track and monitor your performance? How often will you examine your rules and learn from losing trades?

Every strategy could have a different set of criteria that you use in the trading plan; for example, a futures day trade will very likely not have a "defense" to it, or some type of accompanying hedge trade to help manage risk while the trade is live, which is actually quite common in the "Options" world. Tune these criteria for each strategy.


## Making It Yours

At this point most students are rolling their eyes,

looking forward to maintaining "plans" as much as they liked doing chemistry homework back in grade school. Sounds like a lot of work, doesn't it? And how can all of that analysis and paperwork lead to what you REALLY want, which is PROFITS? Well, there's an old expression with cars that also applies in a roundabout way to trading: "A car's not really yours until you've messed with it." Think about that for a second, and those of you who are gear heads will get it right away….over a lifetime you might drive hundreds of automobiles….some you own, others you rent….but a car does not become part of you until you get under the hood and wrench on it…rebuild an engine….replace the brake rotors….change out the clutch….etc. That car then becomes part of you.

So what do you think happens when you "get under the hood" of your trading business and your trading plans? They become "yours," and in doing so, you start to change your Belief System. You start to BELIEVE that you have EARNED THE RIGHT to profit from your trading! One phrase that I say all the time is that "I've never made a dime trading someone else's strategy." I've had to start with the scraps of an idea, perhaps it was someone else's to start with…. and then through this process I've made it MINE. Well, how does one go about building a strategy and making it theirs? Let's see how to do this in the next chapter….

# Chapter Ten:
# Strategy Development

In this chapter, we're going to add one of the most powerful - yet largely ignored - tools to change your Subconscious Mind's response to trading, and with it, your Belief System. We're going to show you how to take a strategy and "make it yours" by developing it. This act of working on something to "internalize it" is one of the most powerful secrets of successful investing, yet few do the work required. Why?

Well, if you're like most individual investors, the following scenario should be familiar to you:

- You learn about a trading strategy from either a friend or some online source.

- The strategy looks appealing because it will either allow you to make money faster than you were before, or it at least looks better than what you're trying to do now.

- You sign up for the program or buy the book and feel that you make a "commitment" to it.

- You study the program and learn it for a week or so.

- They make it look easy, so you surrender to the moment and jump in with your first live trade.

- It does not work out; you lose capital either through the luck of the draw or your lack of knowledge to adequately manage the position through their strategy.

- You hit the books again.

- After a couple of weeks of following their "easy" winners, you try again. You lose the trade.

- The program now becomes "shelfware" as you see ANOTHER program that catches your eye and you sign up for it....

Sound familiar? It should. I would bet that EVERY individual investor goes through this cycle. The reason that you lost money on the trades was due to some basic reasons:

1. **The Herd Effect** - This occurs when a particular strategy or signal works time after time for a while; when everyone finally notices the signal will also correspond to the time that everyone will finally "feel" comfortable making this trade, which means that the professionals will find a way to "fade" the trade.

2. **Knowledge** - You probably learned just enough to figure out how to ENTER the trade, but not enough to know how to gracefully exit the trade with a profit. This impatience on the part of Retail traders is very common, and it's akin to learning how to start a car and apply the gas, but not knowing where the brake pedal is.

3. **Earn the Right** - You had not "earned the right" to make this trade with live capital yet. It takes a lot of preliminary work to develop a true statistical edge for a trade, to make sure that the strategy does provide an edge in the current market ...and that your execution of this strategy is practiced and flawless. You must therefore "earn the right" to trade with live capital and ultimately, full-sized positions.

And to be brutally honest, this vicious cycle repeats itself over and over again while the trader gets more and more frustrated, eventually burning up their capital, all the while blaming others. This is why retail traders tend to "blow out" one account after another.

I know this problem intimately because I allowed myself to get pulled into this cycle, on the quest for the "Holy Grail" of trading, before I got a grip on things and decided to focus on getting good....*really good*...at one thing, and one thing only.

So exactly how do you get good at a strategy? Well, trading is really no different than anything else that's out there....think about any kind of athletic pursuit that you had, like learning to play golf:

- The first time that you played golf, you were atrocious and it really wasn't any fun other than the fact that it was during a corporate outing and no one else was any good. You struggled to make any kind of consistent swing to make contact with the ball.

- If you took an interest in the game, perhaps you borrowed some books from the library or rented instructional DVDs. While your game didn't improve much from sitting on the couch and watching someone else hit, you at least got the idea that you needed to break your game down into different components, like the Grip, the Full Swing, the Chip, the

Pitch, the MidIron, etc.

- You took your practice out to the Driving Range. This was just as frustrating because you would occasionally hit a great shot, but the next one would be a "worm burner." You didn't know what produced a good shot and you had no consistency.

- About this time is where most people seek professional help. You take your first lesson, and while the instructions seem awkward at first, with some application you begin to notice some really positive results with your ball-striking.

- You go back to re-reading the book/video instruction and now it all makes a lot more sense and you can actually start to apply those instructions. More time at the Driving Range now means positive learning and better results. This usually leads to more coaching instruction, and even better results and consistency.

Can you see how this process involved multiple Learning Loops? Each iteration of this process got you to a higher skill level, yet there is no end to the process as many professional golfers can attest to that fact.

So what we need to do as Traders is identify 1) that we are NOT going to be perfect with any strategy out of the gate, and 2) that we need to *earn the right* to trade live capital by demonstrating continuously improving performance as we move through multiple iterations of Learning Loops.

Let's see how we can apply these Learning Loops to our trading business....!

## The Strategy Development Cycle

Ever watch a basketball player shoot a pair of foul shots? Their Goal is to put the ball in the basket, both times. They will follow a routine that they have worked on for years which normally gives them an 80% rate of success. They dribble the ball twice, flex their knees and loft the ball at the rim with their wrist. If the ball goes in with a "swish", they'll do the same thing for the second shot. If the first ball goes in, but bangs off the backboard, they'll apply a small correction to shoot the second ball with just a little less force than the first. This is the application of the Strategy Development Cycle process that we introduced in the last chapter; now we're going to break it down and get more specific on how to use it to build our strategies.

The Strategy Development Cycle diagram that we shared in the last chapter represents the process that you'll need to build in order to become a profitable trader. You'll notice that the cycle starts with "Goals", which can be represented by the distant target that you want to hit. "Rules" represents the strategies and tactics that you'll employ to hit that distant target. Did you hit the target? The "Results" area will tell you whether or not you hit your Goals, and if not, how much you missed by. The final step in the Strategy Development Cycle is "Corrections" where you'll use feedback, analysis, and experience to determine what corrections need to be made in your Goals and Trading Rules in order to hit that target the next time. The cycle repeats, again and again. Professional traders understand how to maintain their development by constantly seeking to improve their execution and results until their goals are met. When they meet their goals, they formulate new ones and go through a brand new iteration of the Development Cycle.

Unfortunately, this is exactly where the average Retail trader falls short. They do not formulate goals other than vague mental ones....they rarely trade via a published set of rules....they do not analyze their results (unless they take a profit in which case they're telling everyone that will listen)....and they most definitely do not make corrections to their strategy. If they do make corrections, it's to switch strategies because the new one that they tried just took a loss. Again, this is why most traders never leave Stage Four of Bo Yoder's Trader Progression that we covered earlier.

## Defining Your Trading Goals

Where do you start to define trading goals?

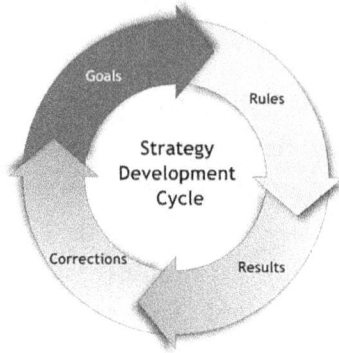

The obvious answer to some would be "profits" or "returns!" Yes, that's certainly one way to define a trading goal, and ultimately we'll get there in time.

One of my early trading mentors was very inspirational; he would constantly pump up his trading team with statements like, *"Come on guys, let's GO! Ten percent a month, no guts, no glory!!!"* Would it surprise you to learn that the many students that followed this mentor eventually blew up their trading accounts? The mentor's goal- setting aggressiveness was not matched by his students' trading skills. The point in relaying this story to you is that it's possible to come up with goals that are entirely unrealistic, even ones that might be dangerous to a newer trader. Setting aggressive profit goals for a new trader is like giving the keys to a Ferrari to a 16 year old boy; just because he has a license doesn't mean that he's capable of handling that machine.

Most beginning traders create goals that are far too aggressive; everyone wants to get rich quickly, don't they? But how do you know what is aggressive and what is not? Do you really know what your strategy will consistently and safely produce? How then can you start by naming a monetary goal? How about your first goal being *just to follow your trading rules?*

Yes, mundane as that seems, the first goal that you need to tackle is to follow the rules that you define in the second step of the Strategy Development Cycle; this cycle starts its life in any strategy as a Learning Loop, so that you can LEARN how the strategy performs in different Markets, different seasons....and how YOU respond to those challenges. Your NUMBER ONE GOAL is simply to follow the rules that you define for that strategy, and measure the performance that you can achieve. Ideally you will start this first cycle in Simulation mode, using tools such as thinkorswim's "papermoney" simulation account or optionsXpress' Virtual Trader.

Unfortunately, most traders do not follow this script. They are in too much of a hurry to start making money, so they shoot from the hip and learn their lessons via "market tuition." Yes, I have made this mistake more than once, so I speak from experience when I say that **your very first goal should be to follow the rules of the strategy that you design.**

If you go through several cycles with your new strategy and you've proved to yourself that you can follow your trading rules and it's consistently profitable, you can now take the next step by trading live. Your position size should be VERY small – small enough that a loss will simply generate curiosity, and not a negative emotional response. Do your results with live trades equal those executed with simulated accounts? Invariably, they will not at first. Trading with live money will introduce new emotions that you need to be able to conquer before you start trading with any size. Your goal for these cycles, therefore, is to trade live positions as well as you did with simulated ones!

Your original goal was to build a profitable strategy by following your rules in a simulated account. You raised the ante by trading this strategy with live contracts/ shares, and your goal was to trade live accounts in exactly the same manner as your simulated accounts. If you have come this far, what's next? The obvious answer here is to shift into a higher gear by increasing your position size, but your goal now should be to "Earn the Right." This is where it's important to measure your performance, and earn the right to increase your position size through demonstrated performance. As discussed in the "Trader Mindset" chapter, your Subconscious mind will act as a "governor" to limit your performance if it feels that you have not "earned the right" to trade in increased scale. Why do you think that most Lottery winners go broke within a short time after their winnings? They subconsciously give it back, and you will, too.....if you don't convince your Subconscious that you've "earned the right" to win those trades, and seek higher returns.

By going through the first cycles of goals, you have finally achieved the ability to start laying out MONETARY goals. OK, now it's time to talk about how we develop the Trading Rules that we're going to use.

## Trading Rules, the Strategy Framework

"Mind control is the result of discipline and habit. You either control your mind or it controls you."

– Napoleon Hill

If you've been trading long enough, you'll know that all the goals in the world are irrelevant if you can't tie them into a strategy to execute against. And if you're using a trading strategy to achieve those financial goals, then you'd better have a concrete set of RULES to trade that strategy!

The next step after writing GOALS in our Trader's Strategy Development Cycle is developing TRADING RULES.

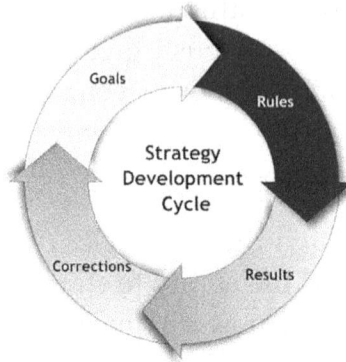

Rules are the meat of every trading strategy that you employ, for if you don't trade by Rules, then you trade by FEELING. Most that trade by feel will trade "with the Herd", meaning that sooner or later a Professional trader is going to eat their lunch. There are some that can trade entirely by feel, however if you dig hard enough into their method, it's more than likely that they've taken thousands and thousands of trades over many years, so that their trading rules are buried squarely into their subconscious minds. They've done Gladwell's ten thousand hours and have achieved Yoder's Stage Six Mastery; so don't confuse Mastery with "trading by feel." To be honest, it's how most of us start trading. We have a GOOD FEELING about a certain stock so we buy it. It goes up (as does everything in a Bull Market) so we confuse luck with talent. A few more good trades like that and everyone is coming to you for your advice. What's your secret? "A *hunch!*"

Most people would rather believe that your success is attributable to feelings and hunches than they would believe that your trading success has been built by religiously following a set of battle-hardened rules. It's an old perception that those that build wealth from the Market have "a gift" or intuition, it's what we're used to believing. After being around professional traders for a number of years, we know better that consistent profits come from tons of honest work and a drive to succeed. No intuition, no special gifts, just good old-fashioned Drive and a mindset of Success. And the Cornerstone of their success has always been based on their ability to develop sound strategies and then follow those rules no matter what.

We encounter all kinds of traders, from those who have elaborate rule sets that are well-tested.....to those that essentially have no rule set. You've all heard that you should "plan your trade, then trade your plan." How exactly does one go about developing these magic rules that you're supposed to trade by?

The simplest answer to get started is to "rent your rules." You should be trading a strategy that fascinates you, that gives you a "rage to master." Unless you have experience in drafting a trading strategy, you might be better off borrowing one; you can find strategies and rules in trading books, advisory services, or from other professionals.

If you're starting out with someone else's strategy, your first goal should be to *Make it Yours*. What do

I mean by this? You have to take ownership of this strategy and the associated rules, so that over time, it will be a different plan from that of the original architect. Why do I say this? Because most traders will "ditch" someone else's strategy and/or rule set at the first sign of trouble. This is Stage Four of Bo Yoder's Trader Progression, where traders bounce from one strategy to another looking for the "Holy Grail." Only by sticking with a strategy that has becomes YOURS over time will you have the faith to stay with it, because nobody has more of a vested interest in your performance than YOU.

How do you "make it yours?" That's the purpose of the cyclical nature of the Strategy Development Cycle. Readers are encouraged to look at the additional online resources that come as a bonus with this book, at the web link listed in chapter Twelve.

Now that you've come up with a strategy and a set of rules to go with that, let's discuss how you can evaluate the Results of your trades.


## Evaluating Trading Results

"It's not what you make, it's what you keep."

– Unknown


The next step after determining Trading RULES in

our Strategy Development Cycle is determining our trading RESULTS; how well is the strategy working, and are we executing it correctly?

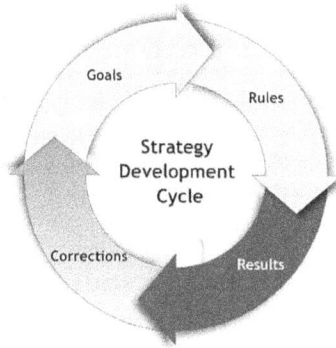

**Numbers Don't Lie.** The first time that many traders start to measure the results of their trading strategy is when they're trying out a strategy for the first time, with live money. That's like buying a $50,000 automobile without test driving it first. Many traders need to just SLOW DOWN and not be in a rush to get rich. Profits will only come after you have mastered the strategy and your ability to follow its rules in a live market. As this statement suggests, regardless of how you feel about this strategy, the numbers do not lie about performance.

This is why we advocate several "development cycles" in the process of bringing a new strategy to market. Not only do you need to learn about, develop, and "tune" your trading rules to make this a profitable strategy, you also need to teach *yourself* to trust this strategy and learn to execute it without prejudice.

The Development Cycle will be different for every trader, every strategy, and every instrument traded.... but it should roughly be conducted with this progression:

**Strategy Development** - Understanding the basic rules of the strategy, developing entry/defensive/exit rules.

**Backtesting** - Utilizing past data, understand the performance of this strategy depending on market type. Tune trading rules as required.

**Replays** – Utilizing past data, test your ability to follow the trading rules in a real-time environment.

**Simulated Testing** – Test the strategy in a live environment using simulated accounts, or in a replay environment. Tune trading rules as required.

**Live Testing** – Using the minimum possible position size, test the strategy with a live account using 1 contract or the minimum possible live position size. Tune trading rules as required, and look carefully for any evidence of "execution gap" where the trader is introducing errors. If trading in this phase is unprofitable, go back one stage (simulated testing) until you're profitable in simulated mode again.

**Live Trading** – Progressively scale in to larger position size as performance allows you to "earn the right." If you are unprofitable in this stage, go back to the "live testing" phase with minimum position size until you are profitable again.

Note how each phase of the Development Cycle gives you progressively greater responsibility based on a merit system; you must "earn the right" to get to the next stage. Again, most traders simply skip all of these steps because they are in too much of a rush to earn their keep and get rich. Instead, they usually just end up spending more "market tuition" fees.

What should you strive for in your Results? The answer is simple – results that match your Goals! Regardless what cycle that you're in....Development, Backtesting, Sim Trading, or Live Trading...your Goals should drive your Results for this cycle. In other words, if your goals for *this specific cycle* stated that you wanted to make sure that you followed every single one of your rules on at least 80% of your trades, what results did you achieve against your goals? By not trying to "eat the elephant" and go from strategy development to live trading in the space of a couple of days, we allow ourselves to learn how we respond and execute each step of the strategy, in different markets. Be patient, it will take time to build and correctly execute a new strategy that you build from scratch.

Now that you have set up Goals, developed a Strategy to execute those trades via your Rules, and now have some Results to show for your work, what do you do with this information? We make *Corrections*!

# Adjustments and Course Corrections

Did you know that a plane flying from Los Angeles to Honolulu is off-course more than 99% of the time? Upper-air currents, weather fronts, and traffic patterns conspire to keep the plane constantly changing its course during the several-hour journey, yet the plane always arrives at the gate within inches of its goal. How is this done? By determining its Goal (destination Honolulu, gate 43), developing the Rules that it will use to achieve this (flight plan), comparing intermediate Results on a periodic basis (GPS/Navigation), and finally by making small but definitive CORRECTIONS necessary to keep the goal on target.

This "servo mechanism" that becomes the final step in our Strategy Development Cycle is really about taking a good, objective look at our results....and then applying corrective feedback to bring the results closer in line with our goals on the next iteration.

**Corrections are Everywhere.** Beyond a sophisticated airplane, this step of observing results and then applying corrective feedback is literally EVERYWHERE throughout our lives...It's why you still need a steering wheel to navigate a long, straight stretch of highway. It's why football teams meet at halftime, away from the heat of battle, so that they can figure out what didn't work in their game plan and make corrective changes to their personnel and play calls.

It's why professional marksmen will correct for distance and windage after a failure to hit the bullseye on the first shot.

The list of examples goes on indefinitely – it's how humans adapt and excel if they are willing to be persistent and patient enough to keep their eye on the Target (Goals) and make enough iterations and course corrections to achieve those goals.

And frankly, *this is where most Traders fail.* You're already one step ahead of them.

Most traders are not willing to go through dozens if not hundreds of cycles through the Strategy Development Cycle to be able to adjust their strategy (and themselves) to be able to successfully trade live in the Markets. We all want results, as do our spouses, and the number one mistake that we see Traders make in this regard is to abandon their strategy after one failed cycle, and substitute it for another as a "Correction." This is where Traders get stuck in Bo Yoder's "phase four" as they eternally hunt for the Holy Grail by bouncing from strategy to strategy.

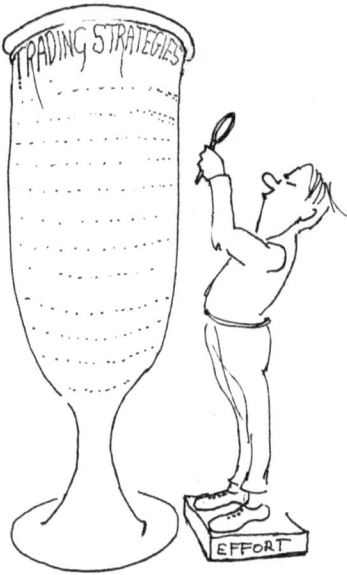

The Holy Grail of trading strategies does not exist...one strategy that works in any market, simply by following lines or arrows that signify trading signals. It doesn't work because we won't let it work; most directional system strategies only have about a 40% win/loss percentage, and the average Retail trader cannot endure the normal drawdowns before the profits come.

Quite simply, we've learned that the Holy Grail of trading is this:

**Find a core set of simple strategies, diversify them to handle different types of markets, and then relentlessly apply the Strategy Development Cycle to them on a daily/weekly/monthly basis to achieve Mastery in their performance, and in your execution of the Rules.**

Again, the reader is encouraged to visit the online

resources offered in Chapter 12, to see many more resources that can help an individual trader tackle the Strategy Development Cycle.

## Summary - Strategy Development

This chapter looks like a lot of work, doesn't it? That's true. Yet you simply will stall out in your quest to advance to the next level of the Trader Progression if you don't take every single opportunity to learn from your performance and make adjustments. This is a very important part of developing your new Belief System, one that subconsciously "believes" in your ability to create edge in the market, and earn consistent profits.

I'm at a loss to remember who said this, but a quote that I've remembered from a pro trader was "I can tell how well a trader is performing by how detailed their trading journal is."

Professional sports has gotten so "over the top" lately where every broadcaster has access to the the statistics of every at-bat in recent history...and can comment on the statistical probabilities with every pitch. Yet most traders don't know what their most frequent errors are. Can you imagine the following dialog?:

*"Next up....here comes Trader Jim. Jim has a winning percentage this month of .545, and a profit factor of .90. Jim generally wins more often in the morning than the after-*

*noon session, and is due for a string of losses that will test his faith in his system.....*" And speaking of the individual trader, let's check back in on Percy to see how he's doing.

# Chapter Eleven:
# Percy's Grail

Percy sipped his warm coffee in the dawn, his room softly lit by the monitor; it was 530am Tuesday morning and everyone else in his house was still asleep. Jenna would not wake for another 90 minutes to get the kids up and send them off to school. Percy was up early because he could not sleep, but not for reasons of worry…..on the contrary, he was restless because he was excited for the day to come and all of the projects that he was working on. It was quite a change from his problems just a few months ago; his new approach had changed his life. And to think he owed it all to three ghosts. Was it a dream or did it actually happen? To this day he was still not sure, but there was no doubt of the impact that it made on his life.

Percy closed his eyes and envisioned the trade that he would take today. The S&P500 had come down to a support level that he had noted in his homework, and the overnight futures showed that this could be an important capitulation point, offering the perfect entry that he had been patiently waiting for. He was ready with the correct options trade if the market opened at this level in four hours. He saw himself opening his broker platform on his smartphone, verifying the price level as well as choosing the right option combination, and executing the trade. He opened his eyes with a strong vision of how he would conduct himself that day, and then began to think about what his day on the job would bring. Since that nocturnal "visit", Percy had begun to re-invest himself into his job again, surprising his management and delighting his co-workers who remembered the "old" Percy.

In fact, everything in his life had improved since his "intervention." He found that the secret was to focus on activities (In trading and at work) that he was truly passionate about. And this enthusiasm spilled over to his home life, which delighted Jenna and the kids. He was much more approachable and engaged with every element of his family.

Percy had taken the time to determine what strategies and trading methods that he was truly passionate about, which narrowed his field of vision down to just a couple of setups that he was fascinated with. He often found himself lying awake in bed, envisioning different ways to create new "edge" in these trades, and it was working. Percy mapped himself in the Squiggle Trader Stage of the Trader's Progression, yet it was clear that he was quickly entering the "Inwardly-bound" level as he was really studying his strengths and liabilities. His relentless focus on analyzing his trade results through Pareto analysis exposed his most significant faults, which he delighted in crushing and eliminating from his trading.

Percy was taking part in a continuous upward spiral and it felt great!

Once at the office, Percy warmly greeting everyone and took a moment to remind himself how much he truly enjoyed working with his friends. At his desk he focused on his job tasks, but took a minute to set

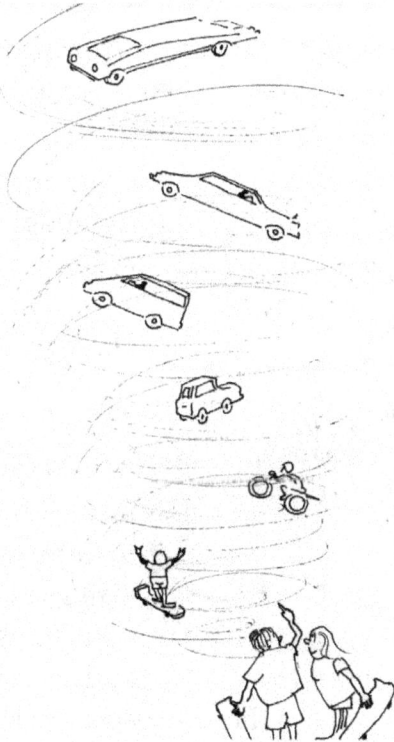

a reminder on his electronic calendar to create an alarm so he wouldn't forget to enter his trade. The trade entry went off without a hitch, and he took a moment to set up a price alert on his broker's platform that would notify him in case the price hit his defensive exit, and he also entered his profit target limit order. He was done with trading for the morning and would not check on the trade the rest of the day unless he was notified to act; multiple cycles of managing this strategy had shown him that monitoring these trades "live" actually created a lower profit factor, so he had changed his trading plan to find a way to eliminate those errors.

After ending his day at work, Percy spent the late afternoon commute home lost in thought about how to improve his defensive skills on a new strategy that he was working on through a Strategy Development cycle. His best ideas usually came to him during these times, and he would grab his smartphone and record a quick voice memo through the voice-activated assistant.

Percy greeted Jenna and the kids like long-lost friends that evening at the dinner table, and intently listened to their stories of the day about work and school. He was truly engaged in their comments and not brooding as before; he was truly "in the moment" for them.

After dinner, Percy excused himself and went to his den, closing the French doors he had installed last month which gave him some quiet without necessarily erecting a "barrier" to his family as he had once done.

Tonight, Percy was excited to review the results of his latest trading cycle and compare them vs. his stated goals from his Business Plan; was he on target? One of the short-term rewards written into his plan, if his 6-month goals were met, was to take the family for a long weekend at Disney World next spring. He literally jumped out of his seat after running the numbers and realized that he had just surpassed his goal and that the trip as a "green light!" He could hardly wait to tell Jenna and the kids, but first he had to check on the status of today's trade entry.

Percy had found his "Holy Grail," and it was located right between his ears the entire time.

# Chapter Twelve:
# Additional Resources

I'm impressed! In today's busy, frenetic world, few people have the endurance and tenacity to stick with the things that they start.....and ultimately finish them. You're clearly one of the "action-takers," and from what I've seen that increases your chances of being one of those retail investors that achieves "mastery" level and consistently pulls income from the market. But before you throw out your shoulder patting yourself on the back, remember that a PLAN devoid of ACTION is just a STORY. You need to turn your dreams into plans and then into results by taking ACTION!

Let's bring everything full circle for a moment. You read the background story of Percy in the first few chapters of this book. Perhaps you might have recognized some of his frustrations and challenges; if so, you're in good company as I see many new investors display these same issues of unrealistic expectations, poor risk management, gambling vs. trading with an edge, and trading from the gut with emotional responses as a result. It rarely has a happy ending if you don't stick a boot in the door to interrupt the corrosive behaviors and modify your approach.

So let's be realistic for a moment; I don't expect you to read a book like this which exposes some of the hidden factors of trading, and instantly turn your situation around and become a profitable trader. The critical factors that I've shared with you in this book came after years of disappointment, frustration, and research, therefore I'd like you to view this book as the BEGINNING of your journey, in which you:

- Achieve a better understanding of how your two "minds" make decisions.
- Start a new discovery process of how to unlock the secrets of the Mind.
- Understand how to train your Subconscious mind for success.
- Learn how to create a new Belief System that has your RAS looking for the right information.
- Find out what style of trading that you're passionate about, and pursue it.
- Determine what level of the Trader Progression that you're at, and what you have to do to get to the next level.
- Build a framework to run your trading operations like a business, including Business and Trading plans.

- Learn how to create and optimize trading strategies using the concepts of Continuous Improvement.

Yes, in theory you can take all of the examples and suggestions in this paperback and for less than the cost of a breakfast at a diner, achieve the Holy Grail of trading profitability. Like the actual process of trading, however....none of this is difficult, but we tend to COMPLICATE it. We make the process tougher than it needs to be.

For the majority of us, we all need help, otherwise it might take us much longer to achieve our goals. Everything that I ever learned about trading, I was first TOLD or WARNED about verbally. True to form, I had to learn things the hard way by making those errors and losing money before I took the warnings seriously enough to learn from them. With that in mind, there are many suggestions and tips that I'd love to convey to you before you have to find out the hard way. Unfortunately, all of those extra things won't fit in this book unless I double the size of it and turn it into a doorstop, so I've put them online for you.

Please investigate the bonus resources that I've created for you at the web page:

docstradingtools.com/grail

And I'd love to hear from you; contact me at doc@docstradingtools.com

Please drop me a note, whether it's a comment, criticism, or a suggestion.
I wish you all the success in the world finding your own Grail!
Doc Severson

# About the Author

Doc has been trading the market in one form or another since the mid-1990's, when his fundamental knowledge of the Tech industry led to great performance trading Tech stocks… however his experience with the subsequent downturn and lack of performance in "professionally managed" funds convinced him that he needed better education in the topic, and to assume command of his own financial destiny. Ultimately he settled on Equity Options as his chosen specialty, and has been trading them as a professional self-directed trader since the mid 2000's. Around this time, word got out of Doc's ability to explain the "complex" and he's been helping mentor other traders ever since.

More information about Doc's free content, trading courses and daily newsletter services can be found at:

http://docstradingtools.com

# Source Notes

i)  http://www.fool.com/retirement/general/2015/01/10/the-typical-american-has-this-much-in-retirement-s.aspx

ii)  https://www.fidelity.com/viewpoints/retirement/retirees-medical-expenses

iii)  http://www.ssa.gov/news/press/basicfact.html

iv)  http://www.forbes.com/sites/phildemuth/2013/11/25/are-you-rich-enough-the-terrible-tragedy-of-income-inequality-among-the-1/

v)  John Assaraf & Murray Smith, The Answer (Atria, New York, 2008) 46.

vi)  John Assaraf & Murray Smith, The Answer (Atria, New York, 2008) 59.

vii)  http://www.forbes.com/sites/85broads/2014/04/08/why-you-should-be-writing-down-your-goals/

www.ingramcontent.com/pod-product-compliance
Lightning Source LLC
Chambersburg PA
CBHW071554200326
41519CB00021BB/6748